The Empire of the Mother

American Writing about Domesticity 1830 – 1860

The *Women & History* series:

- *Beautiful Merchandise: Prostitution in China 1860 - 1936,*
  by Sue Gronewold

- *The Empire of the Mother: American Writing about
  Domesticity 1830 - 1860,* by Mary P. Ryan

Forthcoming:

- *Women, Family, and Community in Colonial America:
  Two Perspectives,* by Alison Duncan Hirsch and Linda Speth,
  with an Introduction by Carol Berkin

- *Votes and More for Women: Suffrage and After in
  Connecticut,* by Carole Nichols, with an Introduction by Lois
  Banner

- *A New Song: Celibate Women in the First Three Christian
  Centuries,* by JoAnn McNamara

- *"Dames Employees": The Feminization of Postal Work
  in Nineteenth-Century France,* by Susan Bachrach

- *Women in the Enlightenment,* by Margaret Hunt, Margaret
  Jacob, Phyllis Mack, and Ruth Perry, with a Foreword
  by Ruth Graham

The Empire of the Mother

American Writing about Domesticity 1830 – 1860

Mary P. Ryan

Women & History
Numbers 2/3

Copublished by
The Institute for Research in History and The Haworth Press

The Haworth Press, Inc., 28 East 22 Street, New York, NY 10010

Library of Congress Cataloging in Publication Data

Ryan, Mary P.
    The empire of the mother.

    (Women & history ; no. 2/3)
    Includes bibliographical references and index.
    1. American literature—19th century—History and criticism. 2. Women in literature. 3. Domestic relations—United States. 4. Popular literature—United States. 5. Women—United States—Social conditions. I. Title. II. Series.
PS217.W64R9 1982   810'.9'354   82-15631
ISBN 0-86656-133-1

About the Author

Mary Ryan teaches history at the University of California, Irvine. She is the author of *Cradle of the Middle Class: The Family in Oneida County, New York, 1790 to 1865,* which was awarded the Bancroft Prize and the Berkshire Prize for 1981. Her survey of women's history in the United States, *Womanhood in America from Colonial Times to the Present,* will appear next year in its third, revised edition. She has been active in the women's movement since the 1960s and is an editor of *Feminist Studies.*

The Empire of the Mother: American Writing about Domesticity 1830 – 1860

Women & History
Numbers 2/3

CONTENTS

The Empire of the Mother

American Writing about Domesticity 1830 – 1860

Introduction

IN DOMESTIC CAPTIVITY:
A DECADE IN THE HISTORIOGRAPHY
OF WOMEN

In the decade since I commenced research on the "cult of domesticity," the topic has undergone a remarkable scholarly development. Perhaps no other aspect of the American female experience enjoyed so much attention from women scholars in the 1970s. Indeed, the nineteenth-century family now occupies one of the most crowded shelves in the rapidly expanding library of women's history.[1]

The preeminence of nineteenth-century American domestic themes is apparent in the programs of women's history conferences, such as the Berkshire Conference, and in periodicals, notably *Feminist Studies* and *Signs*. Perhaps the most path-breaking article in the field is Carroll Smith-Rosenberg's "The Female World of Love and Ritual." This study, which enunciates a major conceptual innovation, the notion of female bonding, is based largely on the letters of nineteenth-century women whose social world rarely extended beyond the borders of domestic life. Many of the other stellar monographs of women's history written in the 1970s focus on the same period and on similar themes. Thus, Barbara Welter's article on the cult of true womanhood, which stood almost alone in 1968, is now flanked by a substantial body of scholarship on ante-bellum domesticity. Nancy Cott's the *Bonds of Womanhood* examines domesticity through the experience of New England women until 1835. Mary Beth Norton's portrait of the largely familial world of *Liberty's Daughters: The Revolutionary Experience of American Women 1750 to 1800,* traces the origins of domesticity further back in time. Kath-

This work was guided and enlivened by close collaboration with a superb dissertation advisor, Lynn Marshall. I would also like to thankfully acknowledge the editorial help of Nina Cobb.

ryn Kish Sklar traverses the entire ante-bellum history of domestic-ity in the company of her engaging subject, domestic reformer Catharine Beecher. This scholarship, moreover, has set the terms for much of the current discussion of women in history; the most recent interpretive survey of American women's past, Carl Degler's *At Odds,* revolves around issues of domesticity as posed in these studies of the ante-bellum period.[2]

This recent literature on domesticity contains extraordinary meth-odological and interpretative innovations. It seldom relies solely on published, prescriptive sources; no longer are depictions of women's lives based on dubious extrapolations from housekeeping manuals, ladies' magazines, and mother's books. Thorough searches through collections of women's manuscripts by Smith-Rosenberg, Cott, Nor-ton, and Sklar have uncovered the materials with which to recon-struct the actual experience of middle- and upper-class women in the nineteenth century. Their favored form of documentation is the private letter and the diary, penned by American women of little public reknown. These new sources, with their personal authority and immediacy, have restored to history a far more lifelike and vivid female personality. Neither victims nor puppets, these new female characters have entered the historical record in a posture of dignity, self-esteem, even power. As a result, Barbara Welter's four attri-butes of "true womanhood"—purity, piety, domesticity, and sub-missiveness—must be reconsidered, and at least one can now clearly be labeled mythical: the ante-bellum women admitted to the historical chronicles during the past decade may have been pure, pious, and domestic, but they were seldom very docile. This is con-firmed by literary historians such as Nina Baum, whose scrutiny of ante-bellum women's fiction reveals a literature reveling in slyly powerful and tenaciously self-directed heroines.

The more specialized studies of family historians have also helped to flesh out the domestic side of female experience. The recent work on fertility and reproduction is especially impressive. Scholars such as Daniel Scott Smith, Maris Vinovskis, and James Mohr have ex-plored the many nuances of the decisive decline in the fertility of American women during the ante-bellum period. It is becoming increasingly clear that women resorted to a variety of techniques, including abortion and sexual abstinence, in an aggressive campaign to control this vital condition of their domesticity. My own work over the last decade has revealed how the women of a single locality, Oneida County, New York, played a creative, self-directed role in renovating the family. The case of Oneida County illustrates the collective, extra-familial, often raucous ways in which ante-bellum women took the initiative in reforming the nursery, the bedroom, and the kitchen. Clearly historians can now acknowledge that women played a central and assertive role in shaping domesticity itself.[3]

Historians also recognize that ante-bellum women were more than domestic, if not in their values and priorities, at least in the spatial and social boundaries of their everyday lives. As studies of social movements and institutions organized and led by females multiply, the parameters of woman's sphere progressively widen. Works by Susan Benson, Barbara Berg, Barbara Epstein, Estelle Freedman, and Keith Melder,[4] among others, demonstrate that women of the ante-bellum era found a congenial and legitimate place for themselves in a plethora of benevolent associations, reform groups, and social services. Thanks to the diligent research of Thomas Dublin, the historiography of nineteenth-century women has also been imprinted with the vivacious image of the mill worker of Lowell, Massachusetts; a young woman who eagerly embraced a chance to escape the domestic jurisdiction of her parental farm family and claimed a place for herself in the factory and the militant ranks of the labor movement.[5] Meanwhile, Richard Bernard and Maria Vinovskis' skillful analysis of the Massachusetts school records demonstrates that schoolteaching provided a relatively lucrative position outside the home for no less than one in five native-born women.[6] We have always known that poor, immigrant, working class women sought and found a workplace outside the home; now, scattered community studies, such as Clyde and Sally Griffen's volume on Poughkeepsie, New York, indicate that significant numbers of the wives and daughters of native-born, skilled and white-collar workers also joined the paid labor force.[7]

When the rigorous statistical analysis of these social and family historians is combined with the sensitivity to personal detail and consciousness characteristic of women historians, the result is a vivid, increasingly detailed picture of how nineteenth-century middle- and upper-class women really lived. At first glance, this swift and robust growth of women's history over the last decade seems to render obsolete a study such as this, a survey of domestic literature which presumes to speak to the actual relationships between women, the family, and society. Yet this study does have a role to play. It seeks to shed light on some of the conceptual and interpretative difficulties that inevitably accompany the accumulation of empirical evidence. In their rapid movement forward, women's history and women's studies in general have stumbled head-on into a major obstacle: the gnarly conceptual problems that lurk in the relationship between women and the family.

This obstruction assumes center stage in Carl Degler's *At Odds*. Degler's argument seems at times like a web of ornate circles spun around the institution of the family. This circularity is apparent in the very title of the book, which first couples the family and women together in some seemingly natural partnership and then depicts the two as persistently "at odds." As depicted by Degler, the American woman was fated to live out her life and history in a half-hearted, self-defeating, but voluntary bondage to the home. American women tasted individualism and craved autonomy early in the nineteenth-century, only to find these aspirations repeatedly squelched by domestic dependency and confinement. Degler describes forays outside the home by exiled spinsters, desperate widows, working wives and daughters, careerists, and feminists. Yet all this energetic movement created only a small eddy, too weak to counteract the circular course of women around the family.

Much of Degler's argument is a synthesis of the scattered conclusions of other historians. Thus he articulates assumptions and concerns common among women's historians of the last decade, including the problematic relationship between women and the family which confronts the reader of women's history at nearly every turn. According to Mary Beth Norton, the legacy of "liberty's daughters" was an "ambiguous" one. The self-esteem and pride of sex acquired in the revolutionary era was soon diverted into domestic channels and converted into more honored and demanding family roles.[8] The "at odds" or "ambiguity" thesis appears in a subtler form in Nancy Cott's assessment of domesticity. Those "bonds of womanhood" embedded in the elegant double entendre of her title constrained females even as they forged the ties of sisterhood, and were, moreover, of a primarily domestic fabric. Cott also discerns, however, that the radius of woman's circle had widened significantly by 1835. Taking off from Carroll Smith-Rosenberg's theme of female networks, Cott delineates a woman's world that extended to the church, charitable work, and informal emotional and social ties between kinswomen and female friends. Cott labels this wider social world "woman's sphere." As of 1835, however, this sphere was primarily domestic, celebrating common womanhood devoted above all to nurturing children and families.

In the process of interpreting woman's sphere, historians wrestle with another troublesome concept—domestic feminism. Daniel Scott Smith, who first employed the term, presents the hypothesis that during the nineteenth century women enhanced their power and improved their condition within the home, without any direct access to external political or social authority. The notion of domestic feminism was soon extended to include the thesis that the cult of domesticity, since it offered honor and relative autonomy to women as homemakers, fostered a positive consciousness of female gender identity, which could lead to demands for further autonomy and even to overt feminism. Without endorsing the term domestic feminism, Cott argues that the sisterhood of elevated domesticity provided a necessary stage in the development of the feminist demand to widen and ultimately dismantle woman's sphere. Other historians, most notably the chronicler of the suffrage movement, Ellen DuBois, contend that domesticity, or a domestic-based women's culture, only deterred women from the public and political path to feminism and sex equality.[9] But none of these variations on the theme of domestic feminism has been put to a convincing empirical test. No one has succeeded in charting the progress of significant numbers of women from domesticity to domestic feminism and on to the feminist movement. It seems on the surface that the connection between the cult of domesticity and the feminist movement is quite remote. While domesticity and a sisterly female culture became fixtures of middle-class womanhood well before the Civil War, the ante-bellum women's movement enrolled only a tiny minority of the female population. Even when female suffrage became a mass movement at the turn of the twentieth century, feminist policy on domesticity was ambiguous. Not even the triumph of women's suffrage in 1920 marked a clear break with either domestic ideology or the domestic attachments of women. Even as women acquired the vote and entered public life, their circular course seemed set by the gravitational pull of the family.

It could be argued that this portrayal of the course of women's history, however frustrating to behold and recount, is an apt characterization of the history of the female gender. There is substantial historical evidence and anthropological theory to indicate that women's secondary social status is nearly universal and associated with their disproportionate reproductive and domestic responsibilities. But to build women's history around a search for a feminist escape from the family is comparable to construing labor history as a teleological progression toward a classless society, or to expect political history to lead to the withering away of the state. Through most of written human history, some form of state and family have provided the basic structures of social life. To pit women and the family in an adversary relationship is an intrinsically frustrating way to investigate historical change. It might be refreshing, therefore, to relax this fixation on the relationship between women and the family. The wisdom of this is already apparent in the vitality of recent studies of women's history that extend beyond the family. Dublin's study, John Faragher's analysis of women and men on the overland trail, and Ann Douglas' agile maneuver across the borders of gender and family in the study of nineteenth-century religion, exhibit this sprightly and refreshing quality.[10]

This is not to say that the relationship between women and the family is unimportant. Indeed, it may be the most important social determinant of gender roles. Rather than presuming that the two exist in some abstract state of opposition, however, it is necessary to investigate the specific historical identity of both women and the family and uncover the delicate connections between the two. In other words, all three terms in this relationship—"women," "family," and "and," the vague conjunction that weakly joins them—demand thorough scrutiny.

The first term, "women," has been thrust into historical debate in diverse and confusing ways. Most recently women have been introduced into history as individuals, the centerpieces and vantage points of historical investigation.[11] But this perspective, which accords the personal account and diary a favored place among historical documents, can lead to historical distortion and has contributed to the circularity of the "at odds" thesis. First, it is erroneous to assume that women enter history as fully defined egos, setting individualized courses for themselves through the external world. The emergence of individualism, male or female, is itself a contested issue among historians. Yet much of the recent history of women not only presumes an individualized female subject, but chooses a mode of documentation that overemphasizes this aspect of womanhood. The woman who writes, and above all the woman who has the time and the inclination to reflect on her own experience in a diary, is likely to have a relatively highly developed sense of self. She may stand apart from the mass of womankind in her claim to autonomy, self-respect, and freedom from the restrictions of the family. Moreover, the authors of diaries and epistles to female friends were most often young, single women suspended between the domesticity of parental and conjugal homes, and thus likely to deposit disproportionate evidence of female individuality and subjectivity into the historical record.[12]

The individuality and subjectivity of women in history must be investigated rather than assumed. The achievement of this goal will require that women's historians cast their net wider than manuscript collections containing the testimony of only a tiny, articulate minority of the upper and middle classes. The full elaboration of female individualism, moreover, necessitates some contrast with the male subjects of history. For example, the individualism attributed to "Liberty's Daughters" during the era of the American Revolution requires some comparison with the pace at which their brothers left parental families, physically and psychologically. Individuality for men as well as women may not imply rejection or opposition per se to the family. Finally, any personal account—male or female—is only one slanted perspective on the past, not its total representation. Until the breadth and the context of women's experience have been more thoroughly researched the image of an autonomous female subject in history must remain suspect: it may have introduced a specious opposition and circularity into the history of women and the family.

Women's history as practiced in the last decade can also be faulted for its narrow focus on the female as context, as well as subject, of history. The most extreme and naive example of this myopia is the tendency of some historians to lavish attention on letters passed between women, while overlooking missives to husbands, sons, brothers, and male acquaintances. This is another hidden danger of an archival, women-centered method of investigation, which sends historians to manuscript collections devoted to females rather than to depositories of letters that passed from female to male and vice versa. Moreover, files of family correspondence generally present an incomplete record of social networks. Because a woman was commonly separated from her kinswomen at the time of her marriage, she was apt to leave a trail of letters homeward to mothers, sisters, and cousins. But the physical proximity of spouses made written communication unnecessary, and hence historical documentation of marital bonds is relatively rare. Here, too, extensive research is required to correct distortions that may have accumulated along with the undeniable advances of a decade of women's history.

The neglect of the heterosexual context and connection in women's history is especially myopic and hazardous. It is all too easy to slip into the assumption that the family is solely a "woman's sphere" when, in fact, it is built upon a heterosexual bond between husband and wife. Even if the nineteenth-century home was infused with feminine values or dominated by the psychological influence of the mother, its fundamental structure was woven of heterosexual and heterosocial relationships. To ignore these relationships would be to overlook, first of all woman's most central domestic function, the socialization of children, male and female. Secondly, by slighting the marriage bond, historians of women casually disregard that critical gender relationship called sexual politics. It is within the relationships between women and men, as well as in the contrast between manhood and womanhood, that sexual inequality is revealed and, in large part, constituted. It is essential, therefore, that women's historians in the 1980s pay special heed to the complex heterosocial and sexual ties that repeatedly criss cross and intersect those two abstract poles, women and the family. To follow this line of inquiry beyond personal archival sources and outside the female experience per se is to regard women's history as more than the collective past of individual female subjects. Rather, it is to study the female side of one of the most significant and pervasive social structures, the gender system.

The limited social space on which so much of women's history is currently focused, the institution of the family, also requires more critical analysis. Within women's history the family is all too often depicted as either a discrete, monolithic institution from which women seek escape, or as a voluntaristic, diffuse, almost natural set of human relationships. The first approach, the one-dimensional rendition of the family as the spatial boundary of womanhood intrudes occasionally into Norton's *Liberty's Daughters* and presents a crude contrast to the author's sensitivity to matters of individual consciousness and experience. For example, Norton uses the extent

to which women worked outside the home as her standard of mea-
surement in assessing changes in women's economic status. In so
doing she fails to acknowledge the many changes in the relationship
of the family to the economy during the period she surveys: such
critical factors as the degree to which male labor was also located in
the farm or artisan household, or the extent to which women's home
labors were linked to the marketplace by the sale of her domestic
production or the maintenance of cottage industries, are hardly
mentioned. These permeable and changing boundaries of the household must be taken into account if the relationship between women
and the family is to have any historical meaning and specificity.

Other historians almost dissolve the family into an amorphous
array of personal relationships. Carl Degler hovers on the brink of
this pitfall when he paints the family as a structureless aggregate of
individuals, seemingly outside the confines of society and history.
"The family, after all," writes Degler, "is at bottom nothing more
than a relation between a man and a woman and their offspring."[13]
Yet, curiously, we are asked to believe that this shapeless, voluntaristic social formation also had the power to set women's course
through history. To put it crudely, the causal power attributed to
the family by women's historians has not been matched by detailed
and specific historical analyses of that institution.

Fortunately, the domestic context of women's history has been
given considerable attention in other academic quarters, within the
distinct specialty of family history. Family historians are compiling
an impressive collection of data on family characteristics such as
household size, membership, fertility, life-cycle changes, and
sources of income. All these measures point to critical changes during the ante-bellum era. Ideally, the work of family historians could
provide a statistical skeleton on which to structure the domestic
experience of females. But individual accounts of women's past experience do not fit easily and smoothly into the statistical framework
of family history. Moreover, almost all the social history of the
family is based on localized studies of places like Buffalo, Hamilton,
Kingston, Lowell, Manchester, Poughkeepsie, Rochester, Rock-
dale, Troy, and Utica.[14] Many of these studies concentrate on one
class or a single element of family life. It is extremely difficult to
stitch together these disparate studies into a presentable composite
portrait of women in the family. They call up visions of a patchwork
female passing from the brash independence of the Lowell girl, to

the fervid maternity of Utica's reformers, to the quiet domesticity of a Poughkeepsie housewife, and then desperate widowhood in some textile town like Cohoes, New York. Still, the urge to construct such a portrait of womanhood is a tempting and not altogether mistaken impulse. The life course of nineteenth-century women, and the interface of women and the family, cannot be located in one moment of the female life-cycle nor in one geographical location. Women hardly remained stationary through the nineteenth century. They participated fully in the geographical and social mobility of the time and were thrust about by social and economic changes which were regional and national, rather than local, in their reach. Still, the history of the family, which flourishes at the local level of investigation and has retrieved a wealth of information, is not yet comprehensive enough to be integrated into women's history without distortion.

We have reached, in sum, an exciting and fertile, yet awkward stage in the conjoined history of women and the family. That history is like an unfinished mosaic, its brilliant particles scattered randomly across a vast surface. The danger is that the sheer sparkle of these isolated pieces will detract attention from the uncharted expanses between them. Thanks to a decade of research we have an excellent view of certain aspects of women's past—the expressive image of a few individuals who left written records, the bold social fact of women's extensive domestic responsibilities, the warm glow of women's friendships and networks. Yet the very brilliance of these images threatens to overshadow other vital elements of the history of gender—among them the vital connection between male and female, the historical specificity and variations in the institution of the family, the dispersal of American womanhood over a vast and changing continent, and the intricate pattern of class, racial, and ethnic differences. To fill in this mosaic and to set it in motion will take longer than a decade.

This incomplete and therefore distorted picture of women's lives in the past requires further attention to literary evidence and justifies a study like the present one. This account of domesticity does not pretend to the verisimilitude claimed by historians of the female experience: it is constructed almost entirely of normative pronouncements, of fiction and myth. Although it may be a tinsel mosaic of domesticity, it at least has the virtue of being a rather panoramic one. Ante-bellum writers wrote fathers, sons, and brothers—the male and heterosocial elements—into their accounts of home life. While this popular literature seldom transcribes the "real-life experience" of any single man, woman, or child, it is also bereft of the possibly misleading idiosyncrasies of the individual subject. Moreover, this literature, which found its way into thousands of American homes, left a relatively complete, visible, and orderly trail through history as one theme, style, or form supplanted or eclipsed another. Finally, literary sources are not subject to the limitations of local case studies. By 1850 domestic literature had transcended local boundaries and conquered a national market. Although this literary rendition of the history of the family and women cannot substitute for social and archival research, it does offer some guidance through the maze of undigested evidence. By virtue of its comprehensiveness and geographical breadth, it can call attention to neglected themes, suggest important moments of transition, and identify the most talked-about aspects of the family and gender system.

I would argue, in addition, that the literary documents examined here are more than vague reflections or flimsy symbols of social realities. They have far more substantial meaning and uses for historians. Widely-read popular literature is a material and social construction, with its own economics and sociology. Culture complies with economic laws, including the relations of supply and demand that had relatively free reign in the American marketplace during the nineteenth century. The supply-side was altered by changes in printing technology, the organization of the publishing industry, and the expansion of the transportation system. Levels of literacy, changes in expendable income, and the whims of popular taste made up the demand-side of cultural economics. The interplay of supply and demand within the competitive marketplace of literary culture created a two-way avenue of communication between the producers and the consumers of ideas and information. Prescriptive and popular literature was the result of extensive communication between writers, publishers, booksellers, and readers. Each party to this interchange contributed in some way to the ultimate content of the most often recited messages. This social and economic relationship created a popular ideology, that set of intellectual formulations whereby a human culture makes sense and order out of the random flow of experience. As ideology, popular literature is an object of historical inquiry as important, and in some ways more complete and resonant, than raw individual experience. It records the way in which that experience was sorted out, evaluated, assigned relative importance, and given a human and social meaning. The depiction of women and the family drawn from these sources does not qualify as social realism, yet it is a valid and intricate representation of women's past.

This study relies on several analytical strategies to extract the full ideological meaning from popular literature. Care has been taken to ascertain the social and economic context from which specific cultural messages emanated. Economic developments at the national and regional level, as well as the mechanics of the publishing industry, provide the economic framework. Underlying social processes are often revealed by a close scrutiny of the changes and rhythms within a body of writing. The elevation of a particular style of writing to popular hegemony may indicate that author, publisher, and reader had arrived at some agreement as to the most interesting, entertaining, or important elements of their common experience. The shrill or obsessive repetition of certain themes may indicate that the writer had hit upon a particularly critical concern of the reading public. This is not to say that popular literature was either a perfect reflection of the mind of the masses or the simple imposition of the publisher's values upon a compliant audience. By situating popular literature in an economic and social system involving readers, writers, and publishers, it is possible to analyze the participation of all three groups in the derivation of a common denominator of culture.

It is necessary, at the outset, to place the cult of domesticity within the pattern of American economic development. The period in which the cult of domesticity emerged and was most exuberantly celebrated—between 1830 and 1860—was a critical era in the commingled history of literature and economics. The rise of mass market publishing, the emergence of "books for the million" as their producers boasted, was but one element in a general rise in American productivity. Economic historians have earmarked the 1840s and 50s as a crucial epoch of economic growth and industrial production. A major transformation was apparent in the large Northeastern cities that harbored as many as half a million residents, the bulk of whom were engaged in manufacturing occupations. By the time of the Civil War the typical urban industrial worker was no longer an independent artisan or apprentice. In Philadelphia, for example, wage laborers outnumbered independent proprieters as early as 1850. The wage worker, the factory, and the big city grew up over the three decades before the Civil War and clearly signaled an economic and social transformation, variously called modernization, industrialization, or early industrial capitalism.[15]

To be sure, the majority of Americans were still farmers and residents of rural areas in 1860. Yet, the speed-up in industrial production and its associated advances in transportation drove a wedge deep into the American hinterland. The most highly capitalized and mechanized industries—such as textiles and shoes—were often planted in once sleepy New England villages and employed the sons and daughters of farmers. By 1840, large cities like Philadelphia shot mercantile tentacles deep into the surrounding countryside. During the Civil War these regional markets would themselves become integrated into a national economy. The area west of the Appalachians was rapidly populated and its open land was swiftly imprinted with an industrial grid—the furrows of steel plows, mechanical reapers and threshers, the tracks of railroads, and the indentations of bustling urban centers like Cincinnati and Chicago. Accordingly, American agricultural production grew geometrically, increasing four-fold between 1800 and 1860 and stocking warehouses thousands of miles away. The American economy took a giant step between 1830 and 1860 toward both modern levels of economic growth and a national scale of production and exchange. If there were any doubts that the breadth of the United States had become integrated into the new economic system, they were dispelled in 1857, when a downward jolt in the business cycle was felt from New York to Chicago and in countless market-towns and commercial farms in between.

Not only crops and commodities, but ideas, too, flowed through the newly integrated and industrializing economy. The rate of growth in book manufacturing actually exceeded general industrial levels. The output of America's printing presses increased ten-fold between 1820 and 1850, and by the 1860s the packaging of ideas and information was varied and lavish. A typical bookstore contained only a few crudely printed volumes in the 1830s; its counterpart two decades later stocked fat novels with gilded edges, cheap romances in bright-colored paper wrappers, monthly and weekly magazines, and ornately-bound gift books. Ideas were launched into the mass market in other ways as well: through subscriptions, the libraries of district schools, through the wares of traveling peddlers, and by exchanges between kin and neighbors. The printed image accompanied the printed word into the bustling marketplace; landscapes by Currier and Ives, houseplans printed in mass by eastern architectural firms, fashion plates by *Godey's Lady's Book,* and boardgames by juvenile publishers all moved along the same busy highways of culture.[17]

The volume, variety, and ubiquity of these commodities testified to the virtuoso entrepreneurship of ante-bellum publishers. Early in the 1820s literary production and sales were largely entrusted to local artisan-printers, whose small shops and skillful hands put out the weekly newspaper, illustrated schoolbooks and hymnals, reprinted Sunday sermons, and sold their wares within the immediate vicinity. By 1860 the local printer was eclipsed by large publishing houses, located chiefly in New York, Philadelphia, and Boston. The success of these publishers is suggested by the current familiarity of many of their names: Harpers, Appleton, Little Brown, Putnams. The founders of these literary dynasties were ingenious marketers who competed aggressively for lucrative literary properties in the United States and Europe. They signed on popular writers with extended costly contracts, and packaged their offerings in ever more appealing and inexpensive containers. By 1860 the pioneer publishers were managing an information industry complete with multistory factories, hundreds of workers, and costly steam-powered presses and binding machinery. These publishing firms operated the nerve-center of the nation and sent messages to the dispersed elements of a vast social and economic system.

The economics of publishing was only the material scaffolding around which a common culture would be built. This process could not begin until a mass literate audience had been created. Literacy had, in fact, grown rapidly between the American Revolution and 1840, when ninety percent of the native-born, male and female, could read and write. With the expansion of the public school system, rudimentary skills developed into sustained reading habits. Millions of American youth became familiar with the printed page, and, through the widespread distribution of standardized schoolbooks, were tutored in a common set of moral and patriotic principles. In sum, by the ante-bellum period native-born, middle-class Americans had been galvanized into a mass reading audience prepared to play their part in the construction of popular culture.[18]

This audience inhabited a social universe that stimulated a hearty appetite for the written word. The men and women who reached adulthood after 1830 experienced American economic development as turbulent changes which uprooted, relocated, and recast customary social networks. Large cities were awhirl with the movement of people changing their occupations and places of residence. In Boston, for example, the rate of geographical mobility was such that half the population disappeared and was replaced within eighteen months. Meanwhile, small eastern towns and farmlands were depleted of their children as the young left for urban areas and westward frontiers. On the western prairies and in "instant cities" across the continent, new social networks were hastily constructed by congregations of relative strangers. Even these new settlements exhibited the pervasive penchant for movement as nearly half of their new residents pulled up stakes again within ten years.[19]

Each movement disturbed and sometimes severed former patterns of face-to-face communication and shared systems of belief. The personal networks that transmitted material and emotional support between parents and children, neighbors and kin, were fractured or dissolved by the waves of migration. Lines of authority were broken as migrants cut loose from local churches, parsons, city fathers, and hometown elites. Usually young and single, the migrant was removed from familiar, first-hand advice on how to till the field, knead bread, or interpret the Bible. The written word was one way of filling this gap and stitching a mass of transients into a society. The uprooted could find company, advice, and solace between the covers of a book. Westward pioneers stocked their wagons with books and subscribed to the same magazines that adorned the mantles back home.

The urban middle class, too, craved literary companionship. Bemoaning crime-infested streets, and haunted by images of immigrants and paupers, its members felt isolated, cut off from society. The middle class was a very unstable and precarious social formation during the ante-bellum era, when men and women scrambled to find secure positions in a shifting occupational structure. Artisans saw their occupations rendered obsolete by industrialization, small shopkeepers faced competition from aggressive regional merchandisers, and farmers were caught in a whirlwind of mortgages, transportation costs, and price fluctuations, while their children turned increasingly to white-collar and professional careers.[20] Such dislocation can be easily exaggerated, yet the fact remains that episodes of geographical movement and confrontation with unfamiliar social and economic conditions had become routine in the lives of ante-bellum Americans. Society was sufficiently distended to create the need for a conversation between thousands of readers and the managers of the publishing industry.

This conversation would in the end create a complex set of literary codes and conventions which, as we shall see, were subject to frequent revisions. Yet, two basic features of this discourse were set early on and would endure throughout the ante-bellum period and beyond. First, publishers, writers, and readers agreed upon the central topic of conversation—domesticity. It was around topics related to everyday family life that popular literary culture was built and flourished. In the course of elaborating these themes, a second major change occurred: the center of discourse tilted decisively along the axis of gender as women replaced men as the primary subject matter, largest reading audience, and the best-selling authors. In short, women and the family were being drawn together as never before on the plane of popular culture. This specific incident in the history of women and the family is the central theme of this study and its point of entry into current historical debate.

The pages that follow will delineate the reorganization of family and gender as it was worked out at the level of popular ideology. Early in the nineteenth century domestic literature was created largely by New Englanders, usually of considerable social repute and with prior claim to the public ear. Prominent among them were Protestant ministers whose homilies on familial propriety were circulated primarily within the boundaries of their local personal authority. In the 1830s and 40s this elite found its hegemony challenged as a steady stream of pronouncements on domestic topics poured forth from the presses of reform associations. For a brief but lively moment domestic values were in the custody of popular-based voluntary associations devoted to causes like temperance. By the 1850s, however, neither local social leaders nor zealous reformers could compete successfully with the managers of the centralized publishing industry. These publishers circulated domestic messages penned by females who coyly introduced themselves to their readers with profuse apologies for seeming to desert the quiet recesses of life deemed appropriate to their sex. By 1850 the publishing tycoon and the best-selling female author had circumvented the localized social hierarchies of the past and conducted conversations on domesticity directly with their anonymous female readers.

The readers' contribution to this domestic literature can be gleaned from an examination of the books on which they bestowed the accolade of best-seller. Changes in the most popular forms and styles reflect and reveal the audience's reaction. Early in the century domestic advice was offered in simple didactic styles and penned with apollonian reserve. By 1850, writing about the family had taken off in two new directions: direct instruction was now the monopoly of specialists, professionals whose family advice became increasingly detailed and secular, while the novel had become the staple of popular domestic literature. The most popular works of fiction played out the themes of familial intimacy to the length of 400 pages and to the delight of thousands of readers. The popularity of the novel, which provided an emotion-charged immersion in an ersatz domestic setting, suggests that masses of American readers had so internalized a set of propositions about the family that didactic instruction was no longer necessary. Domesticity could now be played out on the level of fantasy and imagination. Masses of women became addicted to this domestic genre, with its repetitive formulas and tear-jerking qualities. The convoluted plots of popular novels, which were forever skirting domestic disaster and courting private terror, suggest some of the most grating contradictions in ante-bellum family life and expose many of the anxieties and conflicts endemic to families of the literate middle class.

The literature about the family written between 1830 and 1860 was thus more than a lifeless set of prescriptions about how men, women, and children should conduct their private relationships; it was the liturgy of a cult of domesticity. It had a historical and social life of its own, complete with its own pattern of transformation and internal conflicts. Within this universe of domestic discourse and ritual historians of women can locate those themes that dominated the popular mind and imagination. The readers and writers of the ante-bellum period did not construe the tension between the female as individual and the family as institution as the central domestic relationship; neither did they pinpoint a female battle for autonomy within or outside of the domestic bonds as the major family conflict. The domestic literature which was read so widely between 1830 and 1860 gave center stage to quite another social process, one which was to redraw the lines of age, gender, and kinship in fundamental ways. To put it simply, the patriarchal rankings according to age and sex which were so basic to early American conceptions of social order slowly dissolved and, in the process, social energy was rechanneled into the emotional and domestic bonds between women and children. Although the mother and the child played out their interdependent roles largely within the private family, the consequences of this social realignment were much broader. Under the banner of the cult of motherhood, women participated in the creation, circulation, and generational transfer of social values, thus providing the vital integrative tissue for an emerging middle class. The process was as grandiose as the title one contemporary bestowed on woman's sphere, "The Empire of the Mother." With motherhood their symbolic crown and the home the functional center of their empire women did, in fact, command a critical social position. They were the special, almost exclusive agents of what has been called the relations of social reproduction.[21] The consequences of this cultural use of women's labor were not confined to private homes. Major political issues found expression in the liturgy of the cult of domesticity, and sometimes were transmitted outward into public forums. Slavery, for example became grist for the domestic novelists' mill in the 1850s—most notably in Harriet Beecher Stowe's *Uncle Tom's Cabin*. This particular conjuncture between domesticity and politics exemplifies the political as well as the personal contradictions enshrined in the cult of domesticity.

The first chapter of this volume will describe the transformation of domestic values as it was worked out within the didactic literature written between 1820 and 1840. The second chapter will focus on the pivotal relationship in the new system of values, the connection between mother and child. A simultaneous battle for domestic hegemony as it emerged from the polemics and programs of reform associations in the 1830s and 40s will be recounted in the next chapter. Chapter Four will explore the literary forms that dominated by mid-century, the professional advice book and the novel. The last chapter will examine the impact of the domestic fiction of the 1850s on both personal and public politics, from the bedroom to the battlefields of the Civil War.

As the dramatis personae of reader, writer, and publisher moved about this historical stage, they acted out a very specific and problematic relationship, not just between women and the family, but between husbands and wives and sons and daughters, wherever they met, both within and outside their dwelling units.

Chapter I

FROM PATRIARCHAL HOUSEHOLD
TO FEMININE DOMESTICITY

In the early decades of the nineteenth century small printing shops located in the urban centers of New England and the North Atlantic states spewed forth a steady stream of domestic advice. By the 1820s the volume of this literature had become a small torrent of titles inviting the attention of the nation's "mothers" and "fathers," "wives" and "husbands," "young ladies" and "young men." Should the American reader be unresponsive to so specific a mode of address, he or she might be interested in the more general works entitled "Domestic Duties," "Household Education," or "Family Lectures." There were enough family manuals to supply every member of the American household with ample reading material.

These first expressions of what would become a cult of domesticity were quite temperate in both tone and content. They were plain little volumes prepared by pastors, teachers, and respected citizens, and they extolled a time–honored image of the family; that of a farmhouse or village home, presided over by a stern father and quietly astir with extensive economic duties and social responsibilities which unified its members, young and old, male and female. Yet, this ever increasing body of literature spoke to novel domestic needs and introduced a new presence into countless American households. Information once embedded in tradition and transmitted from parent to child now was conveyed by the printed page.

In the 1840s this prosaic variety of domestic literature was becoming outmoded as the simple, practical family manual competed for popular attention with the more florid style of domestic pronouncement found in a new crop of ladies' magazines. The new popular literature singled out the female occupants of homes across America for special attention and invited them to join in a domestic crusade. A widening network of publishers, editors, and writers courted women with the promise that their loving care and control of husbands and children were essential to the maintenance of social order and public virtue. This message to America's women was often transmitted in glowing domestic images or short dramatizations of everyday family life, not in somber, didactic pronouncements. The new mode of domestic instruction, furthermore, was typically penned by far-flung, anonymous writers rather than the acknowledged representatives of New England communities.

On all scores—in the content of domestic literature, in its tone and style of writing, in the sense of audience, the circumstances of authorship, and the mechanics of publication—these three decades had wrought a remarkably thorough transformation. This change at the level of popular ideology, from patriarchal household to feminine domesticity, was sudden, major, and complete.

Yet it is highly unlikely that the institution of the family, one of the most sluggish and entrenched social formations, could have remodeled itself with such rapid speed; clearly, literary models developed with a lightning velocity that would have left real families dazed and disoriented. I will return to this apparent incongruity between family history and the development of the cult of domesticity at the end of this chapter. My immediate object is to recount hastily this cultural transformation, pausing only to take note of the changing literary forms and institutions which surrounded it.

The first wave of domestic advice, which crested before 1840, swept forward through conventional, often conservative social channels. Early domestic literature was often a simple elaboration of the most time-honored American literary form, the sermon. Typically, its author was the representative of a long and prestigious line of New England Puritans. The Dwight family sent Theodore, son of the secretary of the Hartford Convention and nephew of Yale's president, on the domestic mission. He was accompanied by men of consequence such as Nehemiah Adams, orthodox pastor of Essex Church, Boston, and Heman Humphrey, president of Amherst College. One of the most prolific writers of the early domestic genre, William Andros Alcott, was merely the son of an obscure New England farmer who sought fortune and prestige in the lucrative new field of family literature. Such career calculations were still paying off in the 1840s when the Reverend Horace Bushnell, another farmer's son, took to writing child-rearing literature as a means of ingratiating himself with his middle-class parishioners in Hartford, Connecticut.

These domestic educators presented themselves to their readers in a friendly, colloquial style. Alcott's offerings were typical, "written throughout in such a spirit of fatherly kindness and such a simple style as to win attention and secure an extensive sale."[1] Most family manuals directly professed respect for popular needs and offered assistance to families in the common walks of life. While this literature, taken collectively, had a widespread impact, each work was printed and circulated in a narrow New England area. Domestic advisors of the 1830s used their own family histories and their intimate knowledge of the experiences of their parishioners, students, neighbors, and readers, to construct treatises on home management, child-rearing, family, and society. Hence, the literature of the 1830s appears to be very close to actual family experience, and a grass roots response to ongoing family and social change.

The early domestic literature had outposts along the frontier as well as in old New England settlements. As "Vermont fever," "Genesee fever," and "Ohio fever" carried the American population westward, ministers created domestic advice books for their pioneering parishioners, and western printers reissued the homilies of New England parsons. Utica, in Oneida county, New York, was one local center of domestic literature between the 1820s and 1840s which spewed forth advice to families in the form of sermons, pastoral pronouncements, and religious magazines of Methodist, Baptist, Universalist, and Presbyterian denominations. There was a certain frontier robustness and diversity to this western arm of domestic literature, yet its social base and pretensions were very similar to the New England variety. For example, the leading spokesman of family values in Utica, Presbyterian minister John Frost, had migrated from central Connecticut, as had his printer-parishioners. All were self-conscious partisans of New England traditions.[2]

One ominous innovation in the system of domestic education emerged in both New England and upstate New York during the 1820s and 30s. Daughters as well as sons of local elites began to take up their pens in response to what they saw as the domestic needs of their kin and neighbors. The female scion of the illustrious Sedgwick family, Catharine Maria, assumed this role early in the century. Catharine Beecher, daughter of Lyman, the stern Calvinist patriarch of Hartford, Connecticut, and other New England women of less prominent but equally respectable families, like Lydia Maria Child, soon joined Sedgwick's domestic crusade. On the frontier Protestant matrons took to writing family manuals and editing magazines. Women who took up their pens in behalf of domesticity could not wrap themselves in the mantle of pastoral authority. Rather they presented themselves as servants of their communities, responding to an overwhelming need for domestic assistance. In a preface to a typical family manual, Child presented her domestic offerings as a service for "popular use" among the "middling sort."[3]

These female writers found their way into the fields of domesticity by a circuitous path. In a family manual of 1837, Lydia Maria Child admitted: "If any other than very practical works would sell extensively, I fear I should still be lingering in more poetic regions."[4] A decade earlier Child had basked in literary fame based on her novels of romance and adventure in Puritan times. She abandoned this genre after the great popular success in 1830 of *The Frugal Housewife,* a compendium of recipes and procedures for efficient housekeeping drawn from the author's own domestic experience. Newly wed to a struggling young lawyer, Mrs. David Child had managed a little Boston cottage on limited means, acquiring domestic training and knowledge which her avid and inexperienced readers found indispensable in their own nuclear households.[4] Catharine Sedgwick's domestic perception had been formed in an old American tradition. She was the spinster daughter of Federalist Senator Theodore Sedgwick. Throughout her life she looked nostalgically back to her parental household, inhabited by a host of kinsmen busily occupied with social and political activities. The growing taste for domestic literature gave her the opportunity to reenact her family memories in the form of friendly literary advice.[5]

A similar family history, tested by the fires of a Calvinist conscience, informed the energetic preaching of Catharine Beecher. Beecher also grew up in a busy New England household full of children, aunts, cousins, servants, and long-term guests. After her mother's death, young Catharine bore the heavy responsibilities of provisioning and overseeing a lively household. Her domestic world and personal history were interrupted first by her father's remarriage, then by the death of her fiancé and her subsequent lifelong spinsterhood. Authors like Beecher, Sedgwick, and Child, the first generation of women involved in the enterprise of domestic advice, transcribed their own rather old-fashioned family experiences into the domestic instruction that the New England audience seemed to crave.

The literature that emerged from female and male authors in this period was a potpourri of old ideas borrowed from Puritan thought and improvisations from current experience. Heman Humphrey, for example, issued pronouncements that might have emanated from a seventeenth-century vicar: "Every family is a little state or empire within itself, bound together by the most endearing attractions and governed by its patriarchal head with whose prerogative no power on earth has a right to interfere."[6] In Humphrey's mind "endearing attractions," those affectionate domestic ties, had not yet destroyed the hierarchical ordering of authority. Humphrey admonished sons that they owed strict obedience to their fathers at age twenty as well as ten, while others advanced the age of filial compliance to forty and beyond. Nehemiah Adams, Theodore Dwight, and Horace Bushnell, like Humphrey, addressed their family manuals to fathers and "heads of households."

The New England authors in this tradition clung to older conceptions of the family's relationship to society, as well as its patriarchal internal organization. The domestic advice issued further West was often even more old-fashioned. The religious magazines of western New York state in the 1820s and '30s spoke regularly of the family as a little empire benevolently ruled by a patriarch. One country minister even conducted a homespun dialogue with two parishioners, arguing that women could lead family prayers in their husbands' absence without usurping patriarchal authority.[7]

This early literature inspired an image of the family not only as patriarchal, but as a large, busy social universe tightly integrated into the larger community. No domestic relationship, not that of husband and wife, nor parent and child, was allowed to bask in sacrosanct isolation and intimacy. Marriage was frequently described as a social alliance between two kinship systems, not as the private concern of two young lovers. Lydia Child and Catharine Sedgwick wove the socially extended family into the texture of their early fiction. Sedgwick's didactic narrative *Home,* which appeared in 1837, portrayed the ideal Christian family as one that provided a refuge for domestics, orphans, remote kinsmen, and the neglected offspring of poor and disreputable parents. As late as 1847, Horace Bushnell continued to endorse the old–fashioned practice of "putting out" children. In the interest of the Christian Community, he urged negligent parents to "show your children some degree of mercy by delivering them as far as possible from yourselves."[8] This lingering loyalty to the patriarchal and extended family was often advanced with great obstinacy. According to Humphrey, the family would never change: there is only "one model for all times and all places."[9]

Yet there was both defensiveness and foreboding in Humphrey's position: "The danger is that our liberties will degenerate into licentiousness, and that the growing laxity of family government in this country will hasten the fearful crisis."[10] Many of these early writers could be characterized, like Humphrey, as conservative old curmudgeons, often orthodox Calvinists and Federalists, who reacted to the coming age of Jacksonian Democracy with open disdain. Almost all these authors recognized that an ethic of democratic individualism flew in the face of their patriarchalism. Theodore Dwight, for example, acknowledged the democratic atmosphere that suffused the nineteenth century, but being more optimistic than Heman Humphrey, contended that "free institutions" were compatible with "the pure, simple but exalted state of society established by our ancestors."[11] Dwight, like many of his peers, set out to reform and revitalize the old family order to comply with changing political and social conditions.

This strategic position sometimes gave the impression that domestic writers of the early nineteenth century were walking backwards into the future. William Alcott assumed this curious posture when he addressed an issue that concerned many commentators on the contemporary family, the isolation of the young wife in the nuclear household. Alcott offered what he thought was a novel solution to the problem: upon his marriage a young man might bring his wife into his parental family's house, where she would find both company and guidance in the conduct of her domestic duties. "Why then, do young men as with one simultaneous struggle force themselves away from the parental roof and confine themselves to comparative solitude?" Alcott asked. "Fashion and habit. It has been customary from time immemorial," was his answer.[12] Alcott perceived a need for information and companionship in relatively isolated, newly formed families. He offered the consultation of his books, instead of an extended family residence, as one sure aid to a lonely young housewife.

Thus, Alcott and his colleagues brought advice and friendly companionship to the families within their literary jurisdiction. They presented themselves as surrogate parents, grandparents, and neighbors, a kind of makeshift substitute for the traditional family. In the process these writers described what in their judgment were the most pressing needs of the American family in the early nineteenth century. In collaboration with their readers they determined that the American family needed, first and foremost, simple instruction in domestic management. A series of widely read guides for homemakers soon met these needs.

One of the first such books, Lydia Child's *Frugal Housewife,* was a compendium of seemingly trivial and obvious information. Yet countless women consulted it for instructions on how to bake cakes, brew beer, and kill bedbugs. Beecher and Alcott supplemented Child's manual with additional recipes for food and medicine. There was a home remedy for everything from colds and menstrual pain to the ubiquitous menace of constipation.[13] These books constantly extolled the values of health, cleanliness, frugality, and utility. They served basic family needs quickly and efficiently: elaborate menus, rich food, household ornaments, and excessive decoration were all proscribed.

The wife to whom these instructions were addressed was regarded as something more than a cook and a home decorator. She was a household manager, well versed in budgeting, bill-paying, and bargaining—chores that demanded efficiency, punctuality, and orderliness. In a large family, or one which employed servants, the wife held a position of authority, requiring the ability to "lead, to regulate and to command."[14] It was the continual lament of the domestic writers of this era that, in the absence of cheap and reliable servants, women were busier than ever. Even with the lessening of agricultural chores and home industries, food processing, health care, and household management kept women profitably occupied.

The family advisors of the 1830s did not assume that such important household activities were solely the responsibility of the wife. Alcott advised young men to study domestic economy for three reasons: brides were often unskilled in such matters; the wife was overworked and isolated by home duties; and home management was based on scientific principles of interest to all inquiring minds.[15] The fact that general domestic works were often addressed to husbands and fathers further indicates that the household was a work-place for both males and females, and still retained a patriarchal organization of labor. Women were advised to defer to the ultimate authority of the male head of the household, even in domestic matters. At the same time, husbands were told to respect the wishes of their wives and to regard them as moral and intellectual beings, whose submission should always be "rational and ought to be voluntary."[16] Household labor, as depicted in this literature, was the scene of mutual cooperation and consultation by the husband and the wife, his junior partner.

Yet this literature also revealed that something was amiss in the household economy. Alcott confessed that some women found home life so dull and lonely that they preferred even factory work. "Better by far we should return, were it possible, to the primitive habits of New England," he lamented, where men and women and sons and daughters worked side by side in the fields and by the loom.[17] Other domestic writers had to tax their imaginations in order to contrive opportunities for cooperative family labor involving parents and children as well as husband and wife. Dwight thought that fathers might take their sons to their place of work to learn the family trade as in days of yore.[18] Lydia Child disapproved of the prevailing practice of allowing children to "romp away their existence till they get to be thirteen or fourteen . . . a child of six years old could be made useful."[19] Others felt constrained to state that the husband's work, if outside the home, was not his private concern. Alcott recommended the wife as a "partner in trade," who should at least be consulted by her enterprising mate.[20] The domestic writers of the 1830s recognized, but stalwartly resisted, the emergence of a modern sexual division of labor, which assigned males and females to widely separated work places.

At the same time, these writers often had to look beyond production for instances of family cooperation. Alcott defined marriage as an education—a process of mutual improvement, rather than as a matter of economics. He went so far as to suggest that husband and wife undertake courses in medicine and chemistry together. Other writers suggested less strenuous and specialized programs in mutual improvement—such as uplifting conversations on literary, moral, and religious topics. Even the poorest family might subscribe to one of the cheap family magazines and find therein many subjects for their collective fireside education. Sunday was set aside for religious instruction, the most valued domestic education. Each manual devoted at least one chapter to "keeping the Sabbath." For example, the model family in Sedgwick's *Home,* the Barclays, rushed through their household labors on Saturday, storing up food a day in advance, so that the entire Sabbath might be devoted to religious instruction and worship. They followed the father on charitable missions and edifying walks in the country; they encircled the mother at her drawing board and Bible; they lingered over their meals, absorbed in religious discussion.[21]

These model sermons and family instructions were still placed within a basically hierarchical domestic structure. Mrs. Barclay deferred to Mr. Barclay, and the descending ranks of offspring, foster children, and servants all displayed a clear sense of their family status. Yet, this system was not rigidly authoritarian. It allowed for some egalitarian interchange between family members. Parents even solicited and considered the opinions and preferences of children. Moreover, the formalities of family rituals were often injected with spontaneity, amusement, and copious gestures of affection. Children were nurtured in loving firmness, as well as given stern dictates. Sedgwick attributed the harmony of the Barclay household to the "home cultivation of the affections that spring from the natural and unchanging relations."[22]

While an ample dose of affection was injected into the portrayal of child–parent relations, authors still described the emotional interaction of husband and wife in a restrained and temperate style. When, for example, Lydia Child included the warm letter of Mr. and Mrs. John Winthrop in her chronicle of *Good Wives,* she introduced it rather gingerly: "Those who do not smile at all expressions of mutual affection will find pleasure in the following correspondence." Elsewhere, Child was less sober: "domestic love is the only rose we have left of paradise. Alas! that worldly providence should scornfully cast it away . . . keeping only the thorn as a memento that the lovely blossom can exist in a scornful world."[23] The thorn of which Child spoke was marriage for money, a practice long discouraged both in fiction and in didactic family manuals. On the other hand, writers hardly regarded romantic love as the chief criterion of mate selection. Child advised prospective husbands and wives that the best marital unions were based in shared Christian principles, mutually congenial dispositions, and "a strong, decided deeply-founded preference."[24] The search for the personification of these virtues would constitute a rather subdued courtship. William Alcott added even more prosaic qualities to the list: orderliness, cheerfulness, and business acumen. Alcott appreciated a loving couple, but found exaggerated emotional attachment prior to marriage quite unnecessary. Child concurred in this moderate attitude toward premarital affection. "The greatest and most prevailing error in education consists in making lovers a subject of such engrossing and disproportionate interest in the minds of young girls." Although Child valued marital affection and loving courtship, she thought their development might be left to nature, and did not require literary orchestration.[25] Like the other domestic writers of New England, she accorded such matters a minor place in the curriculum of domestic education.

These family manuals also customarily excluded the sexual relations of husband and wife. The few specialized treatises on the subject subscribed to the same practical and utilitarian values that imbued most of the domestic literature. The austere sexual routine advocated by Sylvester Graham in his *Lectures on Chastity* stemmed from principles of biological utility, which anticipated only vaguely the Victorian obsession with purity. To engage in sexual intercourse more than once a month, Graham maintained, would upset a man's nervous system and endanger his health. Conversely, infrequent marital intercourse was healthy and prudent. "Between the husband and wife, when there is a proper degree of chastity" the sex act produced "no nervous strain":

> They are accustomed to each other's body and their parts no longer excite an impure imagination, and their sexual intercourse is the result of the mere natural and instinctual excitements of the organs themselves—and then the dietic and other habits are as they should be, their intercourse is very seldom.[26]

While more liberal than Graham in his prescribed sexual diet, William Alcott had the same principles of health in mind. He encouraged early marriage because prolonged celibacy as well as sexual excess led to nervous disorders and an excitable imagination.[27] In the 1830s sex was regarded as a necessary biological activity for both health and the propagation of the species, but it was seldom clothed with either romantic sentiments or burdened with the compunctions of feminine purity.

The predictable product of sexual intercourse, the creation of new family members, was the subject of several tracts in this period. Robert Dale Owen's *Moral Philosophy*[28] and Charles Knowlton's *The Fruits of Philosophy*[29] gave the technology of birth control a limited American circulation in the 1830s and 40s. Owen addressed *Moral Philosophy* to America's respectable middle classes, the "honest, upright and pure-minded." He advocated a degree of sexual restraint similar to Sylvester Graham's formula. Both Owen and Knowlton advocated early marriage. Sexual intercourse in marriage not only reduced individual and social tension, but also afforded wholesome pleasure to both sexes. At the same time, however, it tended to produce children who, in poor families and overcrowded households, could not be given the care to ensure they matured into upright and useful citizens. Owen and Knowlton solved this dilemma by proposing that sexual release be accompanied by contraceptive measures, prescribing coitus interruptus and chemical methods as the best procedures. These proposals to limit family size were not widely or publicly circulated, yet neither were they suppressed by overt censorship at a time when notices of abortionists could still be found in local newspapers.

Early domestic literature focused considerable attention on the marital couple and their sexual, emotional, and economic partnership. It tended to downplay the authoritarian rigor of patriarchy and elevated females to a rather prosaic partnership in family affairs. At the same time this literature urged married couples to form binding ties to the surrounding community. Writers such as Horace Bushnell and Nehemiah Adams were most concerned about reinforcing the bonds between the family and the church. Both asserted that families could not save souls without the assistance of the parish. Ceremonies like baptism and regular church attendance were essential public solemnizations of family responsibilities.[30] Theodore Dwight recommended that families cement their ties to the secular community by observing celebrations like the Fourth of July and frequenting public instituions, such as libraries and lyceums.[31] Most family advisors thought that the domestic circle was too confining for any individual, male or female. According to Alcott, marriage should not be a "monopoly" whereby husband and wife relinquish their responsibilities to kinsmen, neighbors, and fellow citizens. He expected each family to maintain direct personal ties with other social institutions: the church, the township, and neighborhood clubs.

Catharine Sedgwick even urged that certain institutions be reincorporated into the family:

> If it were made the practice . . . for those who have homes to extend the blessings to those who have them not, there would be little occasion for orphan societies, and the charity now done by the public would be more effectively done in private families.

In *Live and Let Live,* Sedgwick suggested that perhaps all the Irish immigrants could be sheltered and socialized by domestic service in extended Protestant homes.[32]

Sedgwick demonstrated, once again, the tendency of the early domestic writers to shift suddenly into reverse, and recommend an outmoded element of the American family system as the solution to a current social problem. Yet, in general, this literature carved a rather serpentine, but slowly forward path into the family's future. On the one hand, authors recognized the fragility of the family's bonds to the community and the inappropriateness of patriarchy in a democratic culture; on the other, they clung to both these values and repeatedly used democratic forms of popular writing to champion community and patriarchy.

As the nineteenth century progressed, American readers were seduced by yet another style of domestic writing, one which boldly enunciated a new set of domestic values. Even as Sedgwick, Alcott, Child, and Dwight penned their first domestic treatises, American readers were being serenaded by a new strain of literature. As early as 1810, manifestations of this new style, short, sentimental poems, appeared in small books and local newspapers. When Caroline May collected the works of America's female poets in 1848, she described this body of writing as a typical product of home "with its quiet joys, its deep pure sympathies, and its secret sorrows . . . a sphere by no means limited for woman whose inspiration is more in her heart than in her head."[33]

This flowerly prose imbued the home with gentle emotions and characterized women as a uniquely sensitive, home-loving species. It posed a sharp contrast to the practical and commonsense advice of the family manuals that abounded in the 1830s. Yet the poets whom May anthologized had been proclaiming these sentiments for over thirty years and winning great popularity in the process. The immensely popular Lydia Sigourney began demonstrating her prowess in this medium in 1815. Her poems consisted of a series of anguished laments for dead children, absent husbands, far away mothers, and distant parental homesteads. Anna Maria Wells, whose poetry was first published in 1831, summed up the preoccupation of the female poet:

> Each day, each hour, love's nearest ties
> The hand of death may sever
> And they who live and love the best
> Fate oft divides forever.
>
> Then bend not earthly ties to close
> But let Heaven sustain
> There and there only mayst thou say
> We'll never part again[34]

The biographies of popular female poets offer clues to the social and historical roots of this orgy of sentimental anguish. Anna Maria Wells left her native village during adolescence to attend school in Boston, where she remained for the rest of her life. The popular sister-poets, Alice and Phoebe Carey, lived isolated, retired lives in the West, where their chief diversion was reading novels. The most acclaimed of these poets, Lydia Sigourney, left her family home in her youth for the outpost of the school teacher, married into a family of reputedly hostile stepdaughters, and then fought her way into the social elite of Hartford, Connecticut. These poets, like their reading audience, might well pine away for distant mothers or for the New England villages where they grew up. They also might anticipate yet another uprooting and migration to the distant home of a future husband. While the didactic family writers of the era were entrenched in local communities and often strongly attached to established New England lineages, the sentimental poets represented a more peripatetic, and deracinated population. This genre of writing, furthermore, was almost exclusively the domain of females, denied any claim to authoritative pronouncements on social or political issues because of their sex. The anomalous, often uprooted social status of these authors may account for the fervid intensity and emotional extravagance of their style, as well as their preoccupation with themes of domestic separation.

Yet even the women who enjoyed more settled, established social positions proved responsive to the emotional chords struck by these poets. The biography of Catharine Sedgwick, for example, bears poignant testimony to this domestic sensibility. While acquiring a practical housekeeping education in the cooperative management of her parental home, Sedgwick was also relishing the loving attentions of her father and many siblings. Yet each of her attachments proved ephemeral. Already at age twelve, Sedgwick wrote to her father begging that he turn his attention away from public affairs and back to her.[35] As her brothers and sisters married and left the homestead, Catharine felt betrayed and jealous. She recalled the wedding of her eldest sister (when Catharine was seven years old) as the incident which "gave me early the impression that marriage was rather a sundering than a forming of ties."[36] By 1849 Catharine Sedgwick had converted the emotional traumas of her family experience into a peculiar but apt interpretation of the poetic theme of dying children. "There is a certain satisfaction attending the death of the young— they go before their companionship is essential to us . . . they are secure from changes—coldness—diminution of love."[37]

In the privacy of her journal, but not in her more controlled published writing, Sedgwick expressed her sensitivity to the themes and fantasies that consumed female poets. In her private thoughts the more prosaic fashion of family discourse did battle with these newer, more febrile modes of domesticity.

These competing modes of domestic writing also competed in print. During the 1840s they even vied for hegemony within a single periodical. The *Mother's Assistant and Young Lady's Friend,* published monthly in Boston, recorded the gradual ascendancy of the more effusive mode of domesticity. Early in the 1840s, the *Mother's Assistant* counted men like Heman Humphrey, Theodore Dwight, and William Alcott among its major and favored contributors. These men and other ministers of similar beliefs reasserted the importance of family discipline and filial obedience. This magazine, addressed to women, upheld patriarchal authority and printed articles such as "The Father the King in His Family," which accorded the male status of law-giver and judge.[38] Interspersed with such sober advice and principles, however, were poems in the Sigourney tradition, with titles like "The Heart, the Heart" and "Affection." By the mid-forties such discussions of peculiarly feminine domestic concerns superseded pastoral advice; even New England ministers began to exhibit an interest in matters such as the beauty, love, and influence of women. At this point, discussion of the family resorted to a new idiom. In the *Mother's Assistant,* a vague, rhapsodic, and emotion-packed treatment of home virtues displaced the utilitarian and practical view of the family. Its readers were told that there was "something more than magic in the word home . . . whose very mention thrills a chord in every breast."[39]

The rise of this new kind of family literature also marked the ascendence of a new species of writer. In 1845 the *Mother's Assistant* printed an article entitled, "The Influence of Female Literature on Female Character." The author applauded both the upsurge in women's literary activity and the idea of female character thereby promulgated. Women had "deeper sympathies," "purer motives," and stronger "domestic sentiments" than did men, who were denied the constant, salubrious influence of homelife.

> We conclude, then, that female literature has a special office to fill. Its peculiar task is to address the female mind and mold its character. The time has arrived when literature is to be held responsible to a considerable extent, for the morality of the world.[40]

This article broke officially with previous conventions of domestic literature. First, it shunned the ideal of the cooperative family and a focus on marital partnership in favor of a sexual division of labor. This division allotted domestic affairs exclusively to woman and granted her a distinct temperament appropriate to her new sphere. Second, the anonymous author had the audacity to leap from woman's home sphere to "the morality of the world." With such global pretensions, such ambitions to imperial moral power, female authors conspired to usurp the cultural authority of patriarchs.

Within the pages of the *Mother's Assistant* newly enthroned female writers soon trespassed beyond another literary boundary, presenting their domestic advice in a form bordering on fiction. They wrote short narratives "from real life" which resembled parables and chronicled simple incidents in order to illustrate clearly stated morals. Even clergymen resorted to this genre in recounting the little family dramas of their parishioners. This literature did not present moral postulates and domestic values as the opinions of community leaders; rather, it embedded them in the daily lives of the common people. This amalgamation of fiction, didacticism, and domesticity became the mainstay of the ante-bellum magazines, a cultural vehicle whose circulation increased sixfold between 1825 and 1850.

The most popular magazines of the era, *Godey's Lady's Book* and *Graham's Magazine,* were serving a steady diet of domesticity by the 1840s: sober essays, literary criticism, and European romances had given way to tales of hearth-side marital harmony, and serial love stories. The rival publishers, Louis Godey and George Graham, scurried to attach female writers to their staffs. Godey proved more adept at this lucrative business, securing Sarah Josepha Hale as editor and Sedgwick and Sigourney as regular contributors.[41]

Under the editorship of Sarah Hale, a New England school-teacher-turned-writer to support her fatherless children, *Godey's Lady's Book* molded a new ideal of home life, placing a uniquely feminine sensibility at its center. Hale sneered at the utilitarian William Alcott, calling his prosaic characterization of the housewife "barbaric." The magazine elevated the ordinary homemaker to an ethereal sphere of female power: "Her power is in her beauty. . . . Pure typification she is, of all that is majectic, all that is soft, soothing, all that expresses the one universal voice of love in the creation."[42] This vision of woman, focusing on her subtle charms and abounding love, shattered the delicately balanced cooperative and hierarchical ethic of the family manual. In 1860, *Godey's* alone circulated this feminine image to 150,000 American homes.

Its incorporation into the ladies' magazines created a whole new social and cultural context for domesticity, as woman and family became prey to ambitious businessmen embarking upon the lucrative enterprise of popular culture. Typical of the new cultural entrepreneur was T.S. Arthur, a prolific writer of didactic domestic tales. After an apprenticeship in Baltimore, Arthur set up his own publishing company, invested in others, and launched several magazines. He wrote not as the spokesman of a civic conscience but as an enterprising, self-enriching businessman. Other businessmen-publishers rushed to market domestic authors of proven popularity. The publishing giant, Harpers, distributed the works of both Lydia Sigourney and Catharine Beecher during the 1840s, and most domestic literature was mass-produced on the mechanized presses of similar urban-based companies. In sum, domestic discourse had been removed from the grassroots jurisdiction of parsons and the parlors of female poets to the centralized offices of a national cultural marketplace.

Once it was placed under the management of urban-centered publishers, domestic literature began to depict the family in different social and economic surroundings. The writings of the 1840s focused on the long depression which followed the financial panic of 1837, an event which critically affected readers across the nation. T.S. Arthur's popular tales of that decade, for example, depicted families perennially faced with economic misfortune. In a short novel entitled *The Mother,* Arthur took up the history of the Hartly family just as they were struggling to recover from an economic reversal. In the course of the short book, poor Mr. Hartly suffered a second business failure and a third upward struggle. In 1838, even Lydia Sigourney felt called upon to acknowledge the cold hand of economic change. She feared that "our teeming manufactories should send forth an enervated or uninstructed race—and our cities foster the growth of pomp and elements of discord." Many other authors chimed in describing impersonal and fragmented urban worlds where American husbands and fathers were "surrounded by strangers . . . . without an earthly eye to which they can confide unreservedly their sorrows and difficulties."[43] Thus, while the small town and rural families addressed in the earlier family literature experienced generational instability, the families of industrial cities faced the anxiety of economic and geographic instability within an essentially impersonal, non-supportive environment.

The urban husband, as painted in the domestic literature of the 1840s, spent his working day in that hostile environment. The clerks, lawyers, and businessmen who peopled the magazines returned home only for meals, evening relaxation, and sleep. Wives no longer asked the harassed husbands to participate in the physical labors of the household. At the same time, the growing specialization of men's work made consultation with wives less valuable. One female essayist maintained that no wife "can receive either pleasure or profit from hearing the cabalistic terms familiar only to the initiated in the mysteries of financiering or the occult words and phrases which the professional man employs."[44] The resultant sexual division of labor was described by Sigourney in this way: "the woman's partner toils for his stormy portion of power and glory from which it is her privilege to be sheltered."[45] The division of labor thus defined distinct social spaces, separate spheres for men and women—a "stormy" world for man and a "sheltered" home for woman.

The ladies' magazines of the 1840s seldom spoke of practical domestic skills. *Godey's* told women where to purchase clothes, furnishings, and time-saving devices, not how to manufacture them at home. Domestic manuals and etiquette books put forth shopping hints rather than directions for household industry. Catharine Beecher began to supplement her recipes with detailed health information, long discourses on anatomy, descriptions of home ventilation systems, and the principles of sanitation. These matters were designed to fill a woman's time as well as meet domestic needs. Beecher reported that throughout America women were sorrowed, sickened, and discouraged by domestic ennui and idleness.[46] Female educators proffered young women resources and accomplishments which would keep them occupied when husband and children were absent: "Her acquirements and information may be as companions to her, whiling away the hours of solitude which would otherwise be spent in listlessness, indolence and discontent".[47]

Woman, in the most widely read literature of the 1840s and '50s, was no longer defined by the domestic chores depicted in the family manuals of the past. Rather, she was a separate species of humanity whose distinctive identity was the subject of metaphysical and scientific inquiry. At mid-century physiological and medical writing were concerned with defining female character as well as anatomy. The scribbling doctor, William Dewees, for example, took pains to describe both "moral and physical" distinctions between the two sexes.[48] Alexander Walker's *Woman Physiologically Considered* subsumed the female's mind and morals under her anatomical make-up. He wrote that the man:

> possessing reasoning facilities, muscular power and courage to employ it, is qualified for being a protector; the woman being little capable of reasoning, feeble and timid, requires protection . . . Her qualities of sensitivity, feebleness, flexibility, and affection enable woman to accommodate herself to the taste of man, and to yield without constraint, even to the caprice of the moment.[49]

Although few writers on women would accept such an extreme statement of female submissiveness and intellectual inferiority, most endorsed the characterization of woman's superior sensitivity and affections. Even Margaret Fuller was seduced by this construction of the special character of the female. According to Fuller, women seemed to surpass men in intuitive power, "the electrical, the magnetic element," "the impassioned sensibility."[50] Other female writers were more forceful in their presentation of the distinctive female personality: "the perfection of the female character is completely opposed to . . . the commanding and imposing nature of man." The true woman displayed: "purity of mind, simplicity and frankness of heart, promptness of active character, lively and warm affections, inducing a habit of forbearance and the practice of self-denial."[51] This particular catalogue of female virtues was a distinctive product of the 1840s. Not only feminists like Sarah Grimke, but also commonsense New Englanders like William Alcott, found this a curious contortion of the moral and intellectual identity of the female. Nonetheless, the special temperament of the female soon became a sacred cliché.

The popular books and magazines of the 1840s also cultivated the female's capacity for romantic love. An article in the *Mother's Assistant* had no sooner admonished women to employ "reason and conscience" rather than the "softer emotions" in choosing a husband, than it let fly with the most enthusiastic description of romantic love, "a new charm which spreads itself over existence . . . a peculiar emotion is experienced, the heart has found its second self, its resting place for life."[52] Brief narratives of unrequited love studded *Godey's* and *Graham's,* each piece followed by such simple morals as "don't marry for money," "avoid ambitious and sensuous men," and "don't let false pride overrule the promptings of your heart."[53]

This romantic rendition of womanhood veiled an implicit matrimonial strategy. It seemed to recommend that in the absence of a direct economic function of their own, females spend their time winning and keeping the love of men, whose economic productivity was more certain. In pursuit of this end the *Mother's Assistant* told women to cultivate alluring dress, a cheerful disposition, the flattery of the male's ego, and good cooking. In short, a woman should "make home her whole world." Within the home, the woman's chief activity was to please others. She was to create an attractive home by her "pure and lofty feeling," "charm of manners and conversation," and "cheerful temper." Women's rarefied domestic function was often expressed in metaphors of light. According to

Mrs. Graves, the good wife shed upon her husband's "hours of home repose, the calm, clear light of truth, of peace, and of virtue."[54] Sigourney likened woman's domestic presence to a "dew" and a "sunbeam."[55] Another female poet described wedded love as a "guiding star with perfect ray."[56] Such evanescent images took center stage in the domestic literature of the 1840s, standing in the place vacated by Lydia Child's remedies for the croup and Catharine Sedgwick's formalized family routines.

The love, comfort, and cheer that a woman radiated throughout the home were directed towards a purpose, however, the nurture and comfort of her children and her spouse. Female expressiveness answered Sigourney's query: "How is the head of the household to be made comfortable when he returns from those toils by which that household is maintained?"[57] The wife's conjugal function was defensive and rehabilitating. Its most immediate aim was to alleviate the strain of the man's workplace, usually depicted in the domestic literature as a misty business world, haunted by dim images of stocks, bankruptcies, and speculation. Home repose was supposed to enable the husband "to return with vigor to the routine of his daily labors,"[58] not to urge him on to greater acquisition and entrepreneurial conquest. "Instead of exciting their amibition to place and power, already too active, she should seek to persuade them that true wisdom consists in being contented with the state which providence has allotted to them," one writer insisted.[59] Since a husband's livelihood was seldom secure, the wife was often called upon to assuage the devastation of business failure. Arthur's *Mother* presented the model response to a husband's economic reversal. "We have more than enough for all our wants, she would say—and besides, we have each other."[60]

In the domestic parables of the 1840s the heroine restrained her husband's ambition and cushioned financial collapse. A home life that urged man on to excessive accumulation of wealth and power was universally disparaged. The seduction of the fashionable life was the terror of the ladies' magazine. One female writer seemed to prefer financial panic to fashionable extravagance. She argued that recent economic reversals had served as a "wholesome discipline to a vast number of my country women; purifying, ennobling and exalting them."[61] Not the complicated machinations of capitalism, but the fashionable cravings of America's wives were the customary explanation for economic reversal. Sarah Josepha Hale's moralistic domestic narratives portrayed a wife's lust for the limelight of higher social circles, lavish entertainment, or an elaborate wardrobe, as the force that precipitated her husband's bankruptcy.[62] The ministrations of a cheerful, undemanding wife, on the other hand, insulated man from the tension, insecurity, and corrupting snares of the world beyond the domestic portals.

The backwaters of feminine domesticity were surrounded by a turbulent society. "The fluctuating state of our population, the alterations in commercial affairs . . . the sudden and unexpected reversals of fortune . . . the mania for land speculation . . ." all made of the home a "dwelling place surrounded by strangers."[63] This negative vision of society at large cast suspicion on the ties between the family and the community and discouraged involvement in social and political organizations, especially on the part of the fragile female. "Woman's just duty is to her own family; nor may she leave her home waste and desolate to tend the spiritual vineyards of strangers."[64] Domestic fables traced unhappy marriages and disorderly homes to the wife's involvement in reform societies, her excessive neighborliness, and too frequent church attendance. Likewise, the husband was expected to beat a hasty retreat from his place of business, dismissing his work, male friends, and politics for the safe companionship of the fireside. In the 1840s it was occasionally recommended that the husband vacate the city entirely after his workday. A short trip by rail might take him to a cottage residence on the outskirts of town."[65] The image of a bungalow placed a safe distance from the city and presided over by a loving wife prefigured the modern suburban home—specialized, psychological in function, and isolated from the larger society.

This model home, although removed from basic economic production and isolated from community life, was by no means socially useless. In fact, praise for its social power became ever more extravagant as the new blueprint for a sexual division of labor placed this power primarily in the hands of women. "The sphere of duty assigned to woman considered singly is limited to one family and one circle of society; but the fulfillment or neglect of those duties are extended almost beyond belief." Innumerable magazine articles on "woman's influence" summoned females to their collective social responsibility. These pieces appeared in all varieties of periodicals: religious journals, popular weeklies, and the publications of reform societies, as well as ladies' magazines. Woman's influence was ex-

pressed in elevated but insubstantial rhetoric: "purifying each foun-
tainhead in the sequestered vale of home, that they would send
forth living and refreshing streams to fertilize and make beautiful
the moral wilderness of the world."[66] Writers seldom noted more
direct methods and more concrete channels from the American
woman's home to the larger society.

The theory of domestic influence promised women the power to
set the course of society without leaving home. By sustaining her
mate through the discomforts of his modern work situation, and
gently restraining him from anti-social behavior, a wife did her part
to ensure the national morality. If women's influence was practiced
by legions of American wives upon the vast population of husbands
who composed the work force, all of American society could be
soothed into domestic tranquility. The role of marshaling the solitary occupants of America's homes to this collective task fell to the
female authors, the literary generals of the domestic crusade. In
collaboration with the publishing and magazine industry, female
writers could, by the widespread promulgation of domestic values,
enroll their anonymous sisters in the cause of social integration.

Many women writers wielded their pens as if going into battle.
After warning her readers that a cataclysm equal to the French
Revolution was approaching America, Catharine Beecher asked:
"American women! Will you save your country?"[67] Margaret Coxe
described the 1840s as an age of "morbid excitement" and "disso-
lute excess," characterized by irrational political campaigns, social
agitation by industrial workers and middle-class reformers, and the
moral contamination carried across the Atlantic by hordes of immigrants. Coxe called on American women to erect domestic barri-
cades against these destructive social forces, and thereby assume the
role of "national conservatives in the largest sense."[68]

This grandiose proclamation of the cult of domesticity was issued
before 1850. It was part of an evolving theory of the nature and
function of the family that is remarkably similar to some paradigms
of twentieth century sociologists. The domestic literature of the
1840s contained all of the elements of Talcott Parsons' theory of the
modern family; a unit psychologically specialized, socially integrative, and characterized by the sex-typed allocation of functions—
instrumental to male, expressive to female. Although this abstract
sociological model can be pieced together from the diverse and
scattered statements made by American writers in the 1840s, it

never was stated in clear, complete, and pure form. The new female writers and literary entrepreneurs still competed with the spokesmen of an older, community-bound family system and still held to many earlier ideas and values. As they vehemently resisted fashionable society, they called for the old virtues of frugality, simplicity, and order. Their view of the family as a secluded and sacred domain did not prevent them from occasionally inviting orphans, kinsmen, and servants to cluster around the conjugal hearth. Young women were still admonished to avoid the frivolous practice of novel reading. In the 1840s, moreover, instructions in domesticity still came in quasi-didactic packages, those domestic parables. The prevalence of this genre, with its heavy-handed, bluntly monitory style, indicates that the emergent family values were still in the process of being inculcated, and were not yet deeply ingrained in the public mind.

If this modern sounding notion of the family was still indistinct as ideology at the midpoint of the nineteenth century, it was even more tenuous as social reality. Although domestic writers invoked images of an anomic and alienating society, America in 1850 was still predominantly rural and agricultural. It was, after all, an age of convivial Fourth of July celebrations, ice cream socials, and large farm families, as much as squalid slums, congested cities, and noisy factories. Moreover, young men and women had been uprooting themselves from their parental families and village homes for generations even centuries, without needing to invoke the compensatory ideology of a secure domestic refuge. In fact the cult of domesticity developed between 1830 and 1850 at a pace that was far swifter than the actual velocity of family change. It presented a caricature of family history counterpoising the myth of a strong, extended, patriarchal family of the recent past with an inflated notion of contemporary social instability and individual isolation in the present.

The history and theory of the family as presented by the cult of domesticity was, nonetheless, something more than a nostalgic chimera. The ideology of domesticity sorted out the confusing temporal and geographical variations that characterized family history prior to the early nineteenth century and made a diffuse and extended historical process intelligible and manageable. Even modern historians have found charting the disintegration of the patriarchal family a difficult task. Using as measurements the relaxation of paternal control of family property, changing name patterns, and declining fertility, they have determined that patriarchy was doomed in New England by 1800 at the latest.[69] In the newer settlements and further west, however, patriarchal forms endured longer and declined at their own distinctive pace.[70] Furthermore, any community, or indeed, any family, could harbor both patriarchal and democratic elements. For every son who pulled up roots and established the independent, relatively isolated household that figured so prominently in the consciousness of domestic writers, another was likely to stay at home and inherit the ancestral farm land and his father's sceptre. These erratic rhythms and varied experiences certainly could confuse contemporaries as well as historians. The cult of domesticity, as it burst forth in the 1830s, served as a historical marker, announcing the end of the old patriarchal system and at the same time proclaiming a new set of domestic norms which could carry Americans into an uncertain future.

Popular literature and publishing stepped into this flow of family history and imposed an artificial, but not arbitrary, order on its shapelessness and variety. The changing publishing industry placed greatest attention on these novel and isolating elements of the family. The industry was itself one of the most modern segments of the industrializing economy, and publishing offices were centered in the most rapidly growing urban areas which prefigured modern social and family organization. Finally, as the vanguard of a national industrial network, publishers were particularly attuned to the moving, expanding elements of the vast markets they served. These characteristics nicely meshed with the concerns and consciousness of their major contributors and clientele, women writers and readers. Female authors, especially in the 1840s and after, were themselves a peripatetic and isolated lot, many of whom would never have taken up their pens in the first place were it not for some break in the continuity of their own family histories. Their avid readers, furthermore, often inhabited the more isolated and mobile sectors of American society. The typical reader of domestic literature was probably young as well as female, and hence at that stage of the life-cycle when she was about to move into the strange household of her husband, or confront the anomalous social status of spinster. Either way the young female reader was likely to be especially responsive to depictions of family disruption and promises of domestic power. This fortuitous alliance between young female readers, struggling writers, and publishing tycoons projected a prematurely modern image and theory of the family onto the popular mind. Once that idea had been fully constructed and evoked with the zeal and ritualistic flourish of a cult, it provided the language through which the masses of Americans could interpret their own family experience. After 1840 few middle-class Americans continued to recite the old shibboleths about patriarchal households.

Chapter II

TYING THE MATERNAL KNOT:
1830 – 1850

The domestic writers of ante–bellum America were keenly, often excessively, conscious of the social flux around them. In fact, the central purpose of the cult of domesticity was to provide a familial refuge from the frenetic movement of the American people, to shore up at least one small set of human relations against the forces of change, movement, and discontinuity. Domestic authors recognized that geographic mobility broke the ties between the generations. The typical migrant during the ante–bellum era, and indeed throughout American history, was under thirty years of age, and usually single or newly wed. Before the Civil War, generational fission, both socially and geographically, had become a routine event in the family cycle. Daniel Scott Smith's detailed analysis of one New England town, Hingham, Massachusetts, pinpoints the ante–bellum era as the final and complete dissolution of patriarchal power over the second generation. After 1830 Hingham's families rarely exerted direct control over the movements, marriages, and occupations of their sons and daughters.[1] This definitive break of generational bonds helped to create a receptive audience for domesticity. The cult celebrated and prescribed intense and tenacious bonding within the newly constituted, mobile, nuclear family as a compensation for the network of kin and neighbors which they had left behind. At the same time the cult of domesticity identified, for both parents and children, new methods of tying the generations together with a strength that would withstand even the fractures of migration.

This chapter will describe these new notions of generational bonding, which articulated a basic realignment in the social relations based on gender and age. On the plane of popular culture, at least, the generations were brought together again by bonds of mother love rather than patriarchal authority. This domestic project proved to be a time-consuming and exhausting one; it required that mothers maintain a constant moral vigilance over their progeny from infancy until that critical period when, in early adulthood, they left the parental home. If her maternal tutelage was wise, continual, and loving, a mother was promised that her hold upon her children would endure, however far her offspring roamed. These bonds between mother and child were knit of domestic and feminine fabrics and, as we shall see, were frayed and battered in the stormy world which sons had to face, in the end, on their own. In the encounter between the sons of domesticity and the adult male world, the cult of domesticity confronted its most grating contradictions.

Once again the first energetic advances on this domestic front were led by a band of small-town parsons, printers, and publishers, who commonly spoke in New England accents and addressed themselves to male heads of households. The stern voices of New England ministers resonated from pulpit and pamphlet in the first decades of the nineteenth century, admonishing their parishioners of the "awful responsibility" of parentage:

> It is much to be feared that parents do not seriously reflect upon the nature and importance of the charge committed to their care; they do not form a just estimate of those jewels which God has placed in their possession and immediately under their direction and control.[2]

New England educators and schoolteachers, William Alcott, Horace Mann, and Amos Bronson Alcott, made a hearty contribution to the expanding child-rearing literature. Soon, the expertise of European scientists and physicians, such as Andrew Combe and P. H. Chavasse, was summoned to assist Americans. English and American women writers, including Harriet Martineau, Lydia Sigourney, and Catharine Beecher, also addressed this crucial subject. Because the principles of child-rearing were too sober a matter for frivolous fiction, they were promulgated in the more staid didactic stories of Catharine Sedgwick and T. S. Arthur. Child-rearing in the 1830s and '40s was an eminently practical matter, heavily imbued with the tone and temper of Old New England.

Theological disputes about such matters as the depravity of the child and the practice of infant baptism produced the earliest directives on raising children. As the 1830s and 40s progressed, however,

the nature, treatment, and behavior of children commanded attention for more than theological reasons. Reverend Horace Bushnell's
interest in children was motivated by political and social, as well as
religious concerns. In the 1840s, Bushnell placed his appeals for the
moral surveillance of children in the context of disconcerting social
forces, religious revivals, social agitation, and an aggressive democratic enthusiasm. Heman Humphrey was explicit about the relationship between child-rearing and political developments. Humphrey maintained that "the freer the form of government is, in any
state, the more necessary it is that parents should fit their children
to lead quiet and peacable lives in all godliness and honesty."[3] Horace Mann placed appeals for parental and community responsibility
for childhood education in a similar political context. He was particularly uneasy about the impact of broader suffrage and the general diminution of deference to authority.

> The generation which is to occupy the stage of life . . . for the
> next forty years will act out their desires more fully, more
> effectively than any generation of men that has ever existed.
> Already, the tramp of the innumerable host is sounding in our
> ears . . . . If better care is not taken than has heretofore been
> taken, to inform and regulate that will, it will inscribe its laws,
> all over the face of society, in such broad and terrific char-
> acters, that, not only whoever runs may read but whoever
> reads will run.[4]

Horace Mann turned his attention to childhood in fear of the destructive political and social potential of the next generation of
American adults.

The preoccupation with child-rearing also stemmed from the
more immediate anxieties of individual families. Village and town
pastors spoke to "parents in the common walks of life"[5] who ner-
vously contemplated the curtailment of parental authority. John S.
C. Abbott, for example, wrote his parental guides and children's
books in order to "save some parents from blighted hopes" and
"allure many children to gratitude and obedience and to heaven."[6]
Abbott sensed the origin of parental fears for their offspring. He
followed New England sons into local taverns, out to sea, away to
college, and off to city employment—paths that led away from
home and figured prominently in the writings of the era. The aware-

ness that young men and women would ultimately seek out social and economic status independent of their fathers intensified efforts to form character and nurture morality during their fleeting residence in the parental home.

The progressive decay of the old family economy also encouraged the discovery of childhood in a more positive, less fearful sense. In urban homes and on efficient commercial farms, the child was more than another hand in a cooperative system of household labor. The Reverend Thomas Searle recognized that in this new age the child was not necessarily an economic asset, and therefore must be appreciated for other household contributions: "Children bring a thousand little pleasures and enjoyments to their parents." They were "amusing and comforting," even though a drain on the family's finances.[7] As the child's economic role changed he found new domestic avocations. Theodore Dwight recommended that a son learn his father's trade for his own pleasure and edification, not because of his economic usefulness. Likewise, little girls were seen not as assistant housekeepers, but as the custodians of their own little brooms and tubs, implements of "playing house." The economic asset, the household worker, the diminutive adult, was transformed into the playful child.

These children were by no means freed from parental restraints, however. The writers of the 1830s and '40s did not relinquish parental authority nor rescind the time-honored admonition to obey father and mother. Nor did these child-rearing advisors ignore the biblical command to "train up your child in the way he should go." An occasional New England pastor, such as John Hersey, resorted to the old Puritan practice of "breaking the will" for this purpose. According to Hersey, when the child is emerging from infancy "a struggle is made for the mastery—in which it is to be decided who is to rule—the child or those who are placed over him." The first indication of self-will at this time was to be met with "vigorous measures": a stern demonstration of authority and, if necessary, a solid whipping. In colonial America and seventeenth-century Europe, child-rearing was concentrated in this brief but belligerent episode, which Hersey described in terms of warfare and conquest, yielding "submission" from the child and "victory" for the parent.[8]

Reverend Hersey's old fashioned child-rearing practices were most appropriate to a stable agrarian community where sons inherited their father's status. He acknowledged that these methods would serve "to prepare children to fill your place with honor and dignity when you shall slumber in the grave."[9] Yet Hersey, writing in the 1830s, could not disguise his doubts about the efficacy of breaking the will when parentage did not determine "place," occupation, or residence, for each child. Indeed, a broken will and the absence of initiative it entailed might prove a great handicap to young Americans ejected from the patriarchal household to face an uncertain future and the fluctuating circumstances of an industrializing society.

As a result, the policy of chastening the child's will was swiftly modified. Hersey reduced total submission to "sweet and willing subjection."[10] Thomas Searle advised parents "to submit their [children's] wills to bear a denial; while at the same time, their mind should be left free and vigourous, open to innocent enjoyment and unfettered by the thraldom of fear."[11] Not only was brutal physical repression of the child's initiative discouraged, but love, affection, and mild manners were interjected into the once stern and authoritarian child-parent relationship. Hersey's modification of the practice of breaking the will was a half-hearted response to the new exigencies of child-rearing. Most American parental advisors proposed a more thorough renovation of child management in the 1830s and '40s.

One alternative system of governance already had an honored place in American culture. This was the set of liberal educational practices first espoused by John Locke, articulated in eighteenth-century America by John Witherspoon, and commended to young Americans in the autobiography of Benjamin Franklin. William Alcott's books for young men repeated Franklin's catalogue of virtues and recommended some of his methods of self-improvement, such as keeping a daily journal.[12] Self-governance was a favored term of Catharine Sedgwick: "Again and again I repeat there are none educated but the self-educated."[13] Similarly, Theodore Dwight maintained that "the child must be his own disciplinarian through life." Self-education and self-improvement were premised on a belief in the reliability of the child's reason. According to Dwight, children should be treated "like moral and rational beings."[14] Works in this tradition spoke not of child-rearing or child management, but of childhood education, a process directed toward the intellect of the young American. This philosophy of early childhood education was clearly produced in the waning days of the American Enlightenment. Thomas Gallaudet, for example, wrote children's books full of natural facts, inductive logic, and religious scepticism.[15]

As self-governance relied on the reasoning faculties, it was practicable only with intellectually developed children. But the anxious parents of the 1830s and '40s could not wait for the development of reason to begin their routine of child management. The popular domestic writers of this era, such as Catharine Beecher, seized upon a more rudimentary mental faculty as the foundation of child-rearing: "We do find from universal experience that affection can govern the human mind with a sway more powerful than the authority of reason or the voices of conscience."[16]

This concept of moral education, directed to the emotions and not to the reason of the child, came to dominate the child-rearing literature of the era. One of its most enthusiastic supporters, Heman Humphrey, based his *Domestic Education* on this premise: "*Affectionate* persuasion addressed to the understanding, the conscience, and the heart, is *the grand instrument to be employed in family government.*" Humphrey directed these affectionate techniques toward the "understanding and heart," but anchored them in the conscience. "Indeed till you reach the conscience, you have done little to bind your child to his duty." In Humphrey's system of education the conscience was an ill-defined inner faculty, stimulated by feeling rather than reason.[17] A. Bronson Alcott, an exuberant educational reformer, enthroned this magic concept in his educational system. Conscience was the "primary attribute of a pure and lofty character," activated by feelings, sympathies, and sentiments.

The all-important conscience did not operate automatically. It had to be nurtured from without, beginning in infancy, long before the reasoning power of the child became apparent. Horace Bushnell reported that "I strongly suspect that more is done in the age previous to language, to affect the character of children than in all the instruction and discipline of their minority afterwards."[18] Humphrey was more explicit. He admonished parents to begin moral education between the fourth and the sixth month of the infant's life.[19] Rather than cynically lie in wait for the appearance of depraved passions and then swiftly and brutally suppress them, the parent was advised to gently encourage by warmth and approbation the first signs of inner goodness. The notion of conscience directed parental attention away from external behavior and toward the inner, individual basis of moral decisions. This mysterious faculty within the child, peculiarly sensitive to affectionate stimuli, constituted a critical mechanism of moral guidance.

This deference to the child's special needs was placed squarely in the service of moral control. Attention to childish needs and liberal doses of affection, were calculated to elevate parental values to "dominion and supremacy over the appetites and passions." Horace Mann would take advantage of the vulnerability of infancy to win control over the evil tendencies of human nature. Humphrey guaranteed that his child-rearing techniques would secure parents "a hold upon them [their children] which you have never had before."[20] "Filial Affection" was the "sweetest control" to Humphrey. If parents began their program of affection at four months "parental authority would be established in the first year and a quarter." Alcott described his techniques as "benign and unobtrusive operations" which culminated in parental "power," while Lydia Child labeled her loving nurturance "invisible restraint."[21] Thus, the ideal type of child–rearing prescribed by these authors would culminate in "power," "control," and "restraint." Yet it would reach its object invisibly, sweetly, and benignly, without any child-parent conflict. The subject of this training was left unaware of the sophisticated direction and manipulation of its practitioners. "The child is too young, indeed, to know why it yields, but not too young to feel the power by which its heart is so sweetly captivated."[22] Early use of affectionate moral controls, it would seem, was designed to lodge a kind of portable parent deep within a child's personality, at a psychic location called the conscience.

Child-rearing literature of the 1830s and '40s presented numerous methods of establishing the reign of the parents in the child's conscience. In essence, the design was to "awaken and elevate the nobler affections and pure sympathies of infancy."[23] The first principle of its operation was the imitative faculty of the child. The child was never to have a bad example to copy. Parents should not display anger, viciousness, intemperance, dishonesty, or any uncontrollable passion. Child-rearing literature was peppered with the term "early impressions" which denoted these indelible marks on the child's character. The child's imitative faculty could be nurtured by way of his affections into identification with, and dependence on, adult models. "As the infant advances in strength," Lydia Sigourney advised, "its religion should be love. Teach it to love your own accents, your countenance, your whole deportment."[24] Hence, the magic of the parent's smile would win ready compliance, and the merest sign of displeasure upon a beloved parental countenance would restrain any improper action. The infant would become the emotional marionette of its parents, in a warm and morally salubrious environment devoid of all cause for rebellious self-expression. "If he looks up in the midst of his play, a smile would always be ready for him, that he may feel protected and happy in an atmosphere of love."[25]

As the child's mind developed and his world widened, additional methods of "sweet control" came into play. These were described in children's stories such as Sedgwick's collection, *A Love Token for Children*. The tone and content of these works replicated the moral atmosphere of the model home: complete peace and propriety as a backdrop to the loving interchanges between parents and children, brothers and sisters, girls and their flower gardens, and boys and their pets. The tales inculcated the characteristics of the cult of domesticity: loving obedience, filial affection, peaceful dispositions, ready compliance. Religious instruction was also directed to childish sentiments. John Abbott told parents to familiarize their children with the sweet rewards of heaven and the gentle virtues of the Christ child. To such pleasant tales the child would listen with "tearful eye." The object of the child's religious instruction in the 1830s and '40s was not to fill his mind with doctrine or his imagination with doom, but to "melt the heart."[26] Both the style and the content of this children's library reinforced the reign of affection over the growing child.

The manipulative mechanisms of love nurture are fully exposed in Amos Bronson Alcott's *Conversations with Children on the Gospel.* Alcott's pedagogical method was to "tempt forth by appropriate questions the cherished sentiments of children on the subjects presented to their consideration." He introduced this seductive procedure to his pupils in a democratic, individualistic guise: "If we all think and all say what we think, not repeating the words and thoughts of others, we shall teach each other." Then by subtle suggestions, carefully provocative questions, and his translations of the children's language, Alcott implanted his own ideas in these young minds. Many of these conversations closed with a collective recognition of the power and majesty of conscience. Alcott's pupils parroted his belief in a spirit, the divine part of man that oversees all his actions, clearly labeling them as right or wrong. The children also mimicked Alcott's definition of conscience as a power "over the

unclean spirits within us." In volunteering personal accounts of dis-
comfort or unsettling dreams after doing wrong, these children exposed the operating principle of conscience—guilt. This process is
revealed in the following interchange:

> Mr. Alcott: Yesterday one of the boys behaved wrong and was
> punished. When he came into school yesterday morning, his
> eyes looked large and bright. When he came into school today,
> his eyes are half shut; why is this?
>
> Several: Conscience . . .
>
> Mr. Alcott: The boy I have been speaking of may rise and
> show himself. (Several rose) Well! I thought of one; but con-
> science it seems, has thought of many more.

Alcott cultivated the childish conscience through expcsure, self-
denigration, and public confession. Moreover, in this case "conscience" merely reinforced the dicta of external authority, creating
inner anxiety over some unspecified "wrong" for which the child
had already been punished.[27]

This association of conscience, guilt, and adult control is found
throughout the moralistic children's literature of the 1830s and '40s.
Abbott's contribution to this corpus, *The Child at Home,* is a relentless invocation of childish guilt. He told of little boys whose secret
disobedience made them miserable for weeks; of a little girl whose
hidden crime, eating green apples, was exposed by a "nauseous
emetic." To such homely tales were appended such caveats as "Will
not the child who reads this take warning from it." The tender
consciences of Abbott's young characters were plied with affectionate images as well as the fear of punishment and exposure. For
example, one girl ignored a loving mother's plea: "Will not my
daughter bring a glass of water for her poor sick mother?" This
mother promptly died and Abbott warned his reader: "Your parents
will die also."[28]

This system of moral nurture would, of course, break down upon
occasion. When it did, appeals to affectionate ties were prescribed
as a remedy. The moral education of Wallace Barclay, the troublesome child in Sedgwick's *Home,* abounded in loving rehabilitation.
His childhood crimes were punished by exile from the hearth and
the denial of the warmth of his parents and siblings' company until
he repented. In the interim he served as an example to his brothers

and sisters: "Then learn one lesson from your brother. Learn to dread wrong. If you commit sin you must suffer and all who love you will suffer with you."[29] The punishing parent was accounted the first among these sufferers. A good parent mingled his own regret and pain with each act of punishment. Once the child had begged for forgiveness, and adequately demonstrated his repentance, the affectionate bonds could be swiftly restored: "Let him throw himself into your arms, kiss him, and tell him you hope he will never be naughty again, for if he is you must punish him, and it makes you sorry to punish him."[30] Nineteenth-century child-rearing not only preferred withdrawal of parental affection to corporal punishment, but followed temporary interruptions of the warm regimen with an intensified dose of love.

This moral education all but ignored the intellect of the child in favor of his affections. Moreover, the parents' guides of the 1830s and '40s employed physical as well as emotional devices in order to conquer the child's affections. Writers on child-rearing in this era stressed the vital connection between the physical treatment and moral character of children. Physiological treatises interspersed the tenets of moral education with procedures for feeding, weaning, and bathing infants. Early writers assumed that parents transmitted moral as well as physical traits through heredity; intemperance, dishonesty, and concupiscence were all inherited by offspring. The bloodstream of a nursing mother could carry drunkenness, anger, and lust into the moral fiber of her suckling young.

In the first year of life, the hypothetical, book-reared child enjoyed constant attention and nearly perfect comfort. Physicians and parents summoned all their skills to ensure the painless operation of the infant's physical system. The quality of the child's nourishment, the heat and ventilation of the nursery, the dryness of diapers, the temperature of the bath, and the texture of infant apparel demanded professional scrutiny and constant maternal attention. In all these matters the aim was to maximize comfort and banish irritation. Although an occasional faint echo of older practice suggested a "certain portion of resolution and hardihood,"[31] most books on child care explicitly condemned this old-fashioned practice. Cold baths, wet diapers, and exposure to intemperate weather, all the "hardening devices," were out of vogue.

The first year of the child's life was also the occasion for enlarging his senses, muscles, and morals. Since the infant's nervous system was said to be highly sensitive, strong stimuli like loud noises, bright lights, and overexertion were to be avoided until his senses had been "gently aroused." Sense perception was the first level of knowledge, and, therefore, as Combe put it, the senses should be gradually and habitually directed "upon the appropriate objects till acuteness is gained."[32] Muscular development should proceed at this same leisurely pace. Swaddling was abolished, allowing children to exercise their limbs at will. Rather than pressuring the child to stand upright and walk, parents encouraged him to go through a natural self-regulated development from crawling to unassisted walking.[33] such nurturing of a child's sensory and muscular powers was no idle matter; it enabled the unreasoning infant to imitate and to expect smiles, kisses, and caresses, the key instruments of moral education.

The period of weaning briefly interrupted this gentle process of physical and moral arousal. Throughout infancy the model parent had taken great pains to meet the child's nutritive needs. Mothers scheduled feeding in varying degrees of rigidity but always with the ultimate health and comfort of the infant in mind. The gradual increase in the intervals between feedings, as well as the slow introduction of other simple foods, set the stage for easy weaning. The recommended age for this process varied from six months to two years, depending on the health of the mother and child. The optimal time was usually about one year, or when the child acquired his first set of teeth. Early writers, such as Lydia Child and William Dewees, recommended rather devious and severe methods of weaning, such as applying garlic or black ink, to the mother's breasts. These old severe measures of sudden and traumatic weaning were generally repudiated in the 1840s. If the infant balked at the gradual withdrawal of the breast, the mother should simply disappear until his tantrum had subsided. The infant's happy routine was then quickly restored, side-stepping any open conflict with the mother. Similarly, the control of the infant's excretory functions did not seem to occasion a battle of wills between infant and parents, according to these treatises on the physical care of infants.[34] After infancy, the physiology of childhood became primarily a matter of health and hygiene. Good diet, habitual cleanliness, well heated and ventilated quarters, and frequent exercise composed the warm and healthful world each parent must provide her children.

By the 1840s the construction of this theory and regimen of child-rearing had become a massive literary effort. The cries of parsons in a wilderness of parental indifference had been drowned out by a chorus of popular writers, medical doctors, educators, editors, and parents. The strongest voice among them was female. Women organized themselves into local maternal associations in the 1820s and '30s and thereby quietly usurped the pastoral and patriarchal authority on questions of childhood education. Maternal associations could be found from Vermont to Illinois by the 1840s. Some of their members established "Mother's Magazines" which delivered the message of loving nurture to a national audience. The feminization of child-rearing, in literature and in practice, dovetailed neatly with the gender system enshrined in the cult of domesticity. The true woman was the perfect candidate for the role of child nurturer. She was loving, giving, moral, pure, and consigned to the hearth.

The rise of the mother also converged easily with changes in the conception of the stages of childhood. Since the days of the Puritans the care of infants had been entrusted to mothers and associated with an abundance of affection, even to the point of overindulgence. It was only after the period of infant dependency, according to earlier theories, that mother love had to be intercepted by the more rational and authoritative supervision of the patriarch. This point of transition between maternal indulgence and patriarchal control was effectively dissolved by the theory of loving moral education. The child's moral development was now expected to proceed gradually and continuously from its base in the loving maternal knot. Motherhood had been extended far beyond the woman's biological role in reproduction and the physical care of the infant; it now gave the female parent responsibility for the whole process of childhood socialization.

Between 1830 and 1850 the custody of children was transferred directly and officially from male to female. Early in the nineteenth century John Hersey maintained that the "primary charge of children went to the husband," but within a few decades the father was removed to the periphery of the child-mother relationship. All the newly discovered needs and privileges of children were given into the care of the mother. "And to secure this superintending care, observe what a delightful office the creator has made for the female to perform! What love and understanding can equal that existing in the mother for her offspring."[35] John Searle's description of the pain, sorrow, and grief of "woman's sentence" to maternity was quickly displaced by the sentimental enthusiasm of Lydia Sigourney:

"My friend, in becoming a mother you have reached the climax of your happiness."[36] John Abbott pulled on the strings of mother love, telling the American woman "how much her happiness is dependent upon the good and bad character of her children."[41] The newly acquired emotional skills of the female adeptly fitted her for the mother's role as moral educator, and provided her with yet another object on which to exercise her expressive functions.

Once the mother had been entrusted with the moral and physical care of children, she was encouraged to tie the most intense and enduring maternal knot. Ante-bellum writers were unrestrained in their celebration of maternal bonds, and were even willing to paint them in graphically physical, almost erotic, tones. Breast feeding became a holy rite of motherhood.

> This pleasure does not seem to be the mere exercise of social feeling while the mother is witnessing the delight of the little hungry urchin, as it seizes upon the breast—nor from the raptuous expression of its speaking eye, nor the writhing of its little body from excess of joy—but from the positive pleasure derived from the act itself.[37]

Such an intimate depiction did not seem to cause Victorians any embarrassment. In fact such scenes were even reenacted in the life histories of America's public heroes. Lydia Sigourney even reduced the father of her country to a state of infant dependency on his mother. Her paean to Washington's mother included this vivid image of the maternal knot.

> Say—when upon the shielding breast
>   The savior of his country hung,
> When soft lip to thine was prest
>   Wooing accents from thy tongue.[38]

These graphic images of maternal bonding suggest that ante-bellum domestic writers had not anticipated Freud's notion of the Oedipal crisis. Indeed, they were largely oblivious to the dangers of excessive attachments—both social and sexual—between mothers and sons. They did not express the understanding that children develop independence, initiative, or individual achievement by progressively differentiating themselves from their mothers. To the contrary, ante-bellum writers hoped to foster and prolong children's dependence on their parents. Boys as well as girls were invited to linger as long as possible in the feminine sphere of the home. Lydia Sigourney went only so far as to observe that "perhaps it is hardly to be expected that [boys] should be reduced to the full degree of feminine subordination." Then she went on:

> But is she [the mother] therefore to take any less pains to soften and mould her son to his duty? Oh no. On the contrary, she must take more, and begin earlier. Her toil for him must be as emphatically aimed as the dews of the morning. For by the constitution of society, he must be earlier removed from the influence of home than his pliant sister, and by the innate consciousness of being born to bear rule, will sooner revolt from the authority of women.[39]

Sigourney elaborated her plans for the subjugation of male children in a small volume entitled *The Boy's Book*. She advised the American boy to "beware of the vanity which whispers, you are competent to direct yourselves."[40]

Lydia Sigourney provided one more characteristically extravagant symbol of this principle of domesticity. In a homily to boys entitled "Filial Virtues of Washington," she demonstrated how the knot between Washington and his mother survived weaning. "From childhood, he repaid her care with the deepest affection and yielded his will to hers without a murmur." At adolescence, Washington made a break for freedom, but fortunately this proved abortive. In response to the gentle protestations of his mother, Washington gave up his dream of a sea adventure and sailor's life, much to Sigourney's approval. If American boys aspired to the stature of the father of their country they need only comply with the loving regulations of their mothers.[41] By leaping from the nursery to the presidency with such alacrity Sigourney demonstrated the imperial pretensions of feminine domesticity.

This tight, indeed controlling, bond between mother and male child was at the very core of the cult of domesticity. It demonstrates that the Victorian gender system was not merely the construction of separate spheres for the two sexes. The sexes intersected in such a way as to create, at the level of ideology at least, a tight knot between mother and son. This new twist in the lines of age and gender also created a tangle of contradictions within the cult of domesticity. When those domesticated sons grew up, after all, they would inhabit a public sphere which was deemed the antithesis of the feminized household. The elaborate literary process of tying the maternal knot created unanticipated problems for the boys of America as they journeyed outward from a placid, protective, domestic world toward adulthood in the swiftly modernizing and rapidly moving society. Accordingly, the transition between these two worlds, advancement to adult social status, became a cause of special anxiety within ante-bellum writing.

Although this episode in the family cycle was not demarcated by a term like adolescence, it was acknowledged to be a "critical period," "an hour of anxiety and peril" for parents.[42] An atmosphere of crisis surrounded the educational, marital, and career decisions of young men and women in their teens and twenties. The domestic writers of the era did not recognize and legitimize youthful strivings for autonomy and self-expression which are currently registered in concepts like adolescent identity formation. Rather, they construed youth in largely negative, defensive, and moral terms, fearing their sons and daughters would not withstand the shock of entrance into the difficult and corrupting world outside the home.

This defensive stance toward the approach of adulthood broke with that venerable American tradition symbolized by Ben Franklin's confident exit from his parental home at age 12. Even the heroes and heroines of the early novels of Lydia Maria Child and Catharine Sedgwick were a hearty and independent lot, braving the frontier, Indian raids, and the disapproval of their elders as they set out on their own adventures. Similarly William Alcott's early addresses to youth encouraged a forceful, confident stance toward a seemingly malleable and friendly adult world. In the 1830s Alcott still echoed Franklin, saying "man as a general rule, becomes whatever he desires even later in life."[43] During the 1840s, however, the likes of Catharine Beecher's young brother, Henry Ward, appointed themselves advisors to youth, and painted the transition to adulthood in menacing colors. Beecher warned young men that they were embarking on a world of "snares and temptations," populated by "spiders" and "monsters," who lured unsuspecting youth into gambling houses, brothels, taverns, indecent theaters, and dens of iniquity rather than shrines of domesticity.

A bevy of other writers picked up Beecher's theme as they alerted youth and parents to the hostile, incomprehensible, fluctuating world outside the home. The popular tales of Fanny Forrester, for example, commonly began as a young man or woman departed from a cozy rural cottage and made his or her way to some distant city. Forrester's male counterpart, Lucius Sargent, was fond of portraying the same scene, as well as recounting how a young man returned home in later life only to find the old homestead gone, nary a trace of friends and relatives, and the town overrun with strangers, factories, and cold-hearted businessmen. The lectures to young men which moralists such as Beecher and Horace Mann delivered in lyceums and public halls across America also repeatedly shifted the social setting of their tales from farm to village to city.

All these authors gave in to one reflexive response to the crisis of youth—to beat a retreat homeward. As wicked men beckoned village sons into the adult world, Beecher was known to shout, "Scurry home" and "bolt the door." The domestic stories of the 1840s were also fond of describing prodigal sons and daughters who returned crestfallen to their mothers and fathers after a disastrous trial and failure in the city.[44]

Historians have accumulated statistical evidence that in places like Hamilton, Ontario, and Utica, New York, the sons and daughters of the middle class were in fact more reluctant to leave their parental homes at mid-century than in the past. By the 1860s as many as 40 percent of the young men in their late twenties in these communities still resided with their parents.[45] This longer residence under the parental roof not only extended the period of moral control by the mother but also allowed parents to supervise the social transitions incumbent on young adults. In the literature of the ante-bellum era, these critical transitions varied according to the sex of the child; predictably, the young female's major social decision was choosing a husband, the male's, securing a job.

The young woman's goal was seen as relatively free of conflict. After all, she was destined merely to vacate one home for another, to relocate her domestic affections and home duties in a household headed by her husband rather than her father. The psychic difficulties of this transition were not inconsiderable, however, and were often the theme of moralistic women's fiction. Catharine Sedgwick's heroine, Gertrude Clarence, mirrored many a nineteenth-century woman in her struggle to detach her affection from her father and affix it to a young man. Gradually Gertrude came to realize that "my father is all a father can be to me, but for perfect sympathy there must be a similar age, pursuits, and hopes." The sexual barrier women vaulted at the time of marriage was even more formidable. Both fiction and actual correspondence between mothers and their married daughters testified to the wrenching, often incomplete, transfer of affection from mother to spouse.[46]

This literature was rarely concerned with posing occupational alternatives to marriage, child-rearing, and housewifery. Young women were warned, however, that they should be prepared for fluctuations in the social and economic status of their husbands-to-be. A woman should equip herself with the domestic skills necessary in a poor and servantless home, as well as the elegance and taste required to adorn a rich man's mansion. Training in some other respectable skill like needlework or teaching would allow her to support herself in spinsterhood or widowhood. Young women were not encouraged, however, to take their futures directly in their own hands. Rather, as Lydia Sigourney put it, a good female education "makes us content with our lot," and "teaches in any situation how to be happy."[47] Margaret Graves warned women that in matters of love and work "self dependence and self-control are ever the offspring of weakness and ignorance."[48] Behind the scenes, it was the parents who orchestrated the critical marital decisions of young women. For example, in T.S. Arthur's *The Mother,* Mary Hartley was secluded from male society until she was eighteen, and then her associates were scrutinized in order to screen out anyone but a correct, parentally-approved marriage partner.

For the male, the prospective breadwinner, such ambiguous preparations for the future were inadequate. Yet he, too, was offered few concrete career guidelines. Early in the century William Alcott sent the young New England villager off into the world with the simple skills and virtues of a merchant capitalist: industry, frugality, honesty, good accounting, and the disposition to pay debts promptly. These character traits and business practices would serve independent farmers, shopkeepers, and craftsmen well or might aid ingenious young men seeking their fortunes in industry.[49] In 1830 Catharine Sedgwick made an industrialist the hero of *Clarence,* but his fictional colleagues were few in the decades that

followed. Fanny Forrester appreciatively reported one hero's rejection of his father's risky manufacturing business to become a comfortable lawyer.[50] Industrial entrepreneur was not a role generally
recommended for American youth in the 1830s and '40s.

Horace Mann's *A Few Thoughts for Young Men* focused on the
dangers inherent in an ambitious career choice. These were lectures
delivered before the Boston Mercantile Library Association, a
group composed of clerks employed in mercantile houses, broker-
age firms, and retail stores. Mann offered few incentives to dramatic
upward mobility. For young men "torn from the parental stock and
transplanted in the city, there are few higher earthly duties than to
obtain a competency." Thus Mann instructed young men in the
virtues of sobriety, diligence, abstinence from pleasure, and general
caution rather than entrepreneurial daring or specific business
skills.[51] Henry Ward Beecher's lectures also were addressed to employees, not aspiring independent businessmen. In a section entitled, "Relations to Employers," Beecher discouraged his young audience from regarding their bosses simply as men "who for the time
being, have an advantage over you, or in some sense are your
instruments, or are obstacles in your way." The employer was
rather a fellow Christian whom the young man was duty-bound to
serve faithfully and constantly.[52] Young men were advised to fulfill
the responsibilities of wage-earners and not usurp the employer's
power and position.

Neither Beecher nor Mann recommended advancement from the
status of employee to that of employer. They portrayed the upper
ranks of the business world as morally dangerous and economically
insecure. Beecher used his most forbidding and paranoid rhetoric in
describing the business world: a "mania of dishonesty," abounding
in "absconding agents, swindling schemes, and defalcations," "an
ocean deluge of dishonesty and crime, which has been sweeping
over the whole land." In addition "every few years commerce has
its earthquakes." Bankruptcy, a seemingly inevitable occupational
hazard, was a horrifying spectacle: creditors rush upon the debtor
"like wolves upon a wounded deer, dragging him down, ripping him
open, breast to flank, plunging deep their bloody muzzles to reach
the heart and taste blood at the very fountain." A youth might well
have second thoughts about entering this world of vampires and
cannibals. At the very least, he should approach it with caution and
moderate aspirations.

> If our young men are introduced to life with distaste for safe ways, because the sure profits are slow: if the opinion becomes prevalent that all business is great, only as it tends to the uncertain, the extravagant, and the romantic; then we may stay our hand at once, nor waste labor in the absurd expostulations of honesty.[53]

"Safety" and "competency" as employees, not aggressive and risk-taking entrepreneurship were the occupational ambitions Beecher recommended to the first generation to inhabit industrial America.

In the age of protective child-rearing, however, career decisions were not entirely the concern of the young. The intuitive powers of the all-attentive mother equipped her to be her son's career counselor. She could "encourage ardent desires of the youthful mind, and confirm those traits by which professional pursuits might be hereafter decided."[54] Some mothers might seek the assistance of a phrenologist in finding a career appropriate to the terrain of her child's skull. Families like the Hartleys soberly determined the occupation most appropriate to their children's temperaments. Each family, moreover, was expected to provide a home environment destructive to greedy and adventurous aspirations. In fact, parents would do well to limit their own ambition, to rest in the tranquil world of the "middling sort," so as to afford a proper model of moderation to their children. Career decisions, like the solutions to all the dilemmas of youth, were still considered within the purview of parents.

Yet even the most enthusiastic supporters of this extended parental surveillance had to admit that the fathers and mothers of the ante-bellum era were relatively powerless at this moment of greatest domestic trial, when a youth confronted the adult problem of earning a living. Lydia Child put it this way:

> It is certainly very desirable to fit children for the status they are likely to fill, as far as a parent can judge what that station will be. In this country, it is a difficult point to decide: for one half our people are in a totally different situation from what might have been expected in their childhood.[55]

It was the rare child indeed who simply inherited his father's farm, workshop, or retail establishment after 1830. And even if he did, he would have to make his way in an increasingly competitive and

erratic marketplace. Since a high school, much less a college, education was rare before the Civil War, and training for the professions
was unsystematic, few parents could plant their sons very securely
on the path to occupational success.

The material circumstances and moral pitfalls that awaited children outside their parental homes were not always amenable to
maternal intervention. As a consequence, many mothers watched
with passive trepidation as their sons departed from home. Fanny
Forrester gave voice to a mother's worries in the following lines:

> Her first born, her only son, the darling of her young heart,
> her pride in the first years of wedded life, he whom she had
> loved so fondly and cherished so tenderly—to what vice, what
> suffering might he be exposed.[56]

These anxieties, built into the very center of the ante-bellum family
and gender system, were not easily allayed, not even by the lofty
phrases and ebullient promises of the cult of domesticity.

These anxieties did, however, find a forum for literary expression
and perhaps personal catharsis. A hearty literary genre of the 1840s,
the temperance tale, was little more than a distillation of these
contradictions of the maternal knot. The problem of sending home-
sheltered young men and women into an increasingly complex society, did not invite simple, sermonlike tales. Amid the confusion and
unpredictability of a youth's entrance into larger society, the plots
were complicated and happy endings were not assured. The victims
in these tales of intemperance were from both rich and poor families
and were the products of all varieties of child care: fashionable
neglect, brutal breaking of the will, and overindulgence, as well as
loving firmness. The multifarious tragedies of this literature exposed
the precarious posture of the American family in the 1840s, as it
tried to mediate home and society.

The plots of temperance tales revolved around the sundry pitfalls
of youth. Sargent's "Margaret's Bridal," for example, presented the
problems of the young female as the products of intemperance.
Margaret had pledged heart and hand to a young man about to
depart for college. As was often the case in these tales, college
became the scene of the youth's decline into intemperance. Upon
learning of her beloved's fall, Margaret stoically decided to break
the engagement, but the pleas of the drunkard's mother soon con-

vinced her that her love alone would reform the unfortunate inebriate. Consequently the alliance was reestablished, the intemperate reformed, and the wedding celebrated. Yet the plot did not end at this romantic juncture. Margaret's temperance principles did not extend to total abstinence from all intoxicating beverages. In the course of the wedding celebration the unsuspecting bride offered her new spouse a cup of wine, bringing on a tragic denouement of drunkenness and death.[57]

Temperance literature expressed the complicated crisis of the young female. She appeared in the guise of victim, temptress, and drunkard. Many a tragic heroine saw her marital hopes consumed in a quaff of liquor. A poem by Alice Carey presented the plight of the betrothed awaiting the return of her fiancé from a year in the city. Exposed to "life's conflict and its care," her young man succumbed to alcoholism, crime, and the gallows. "He is a convict doomed to die," "I with a bleeding broken heart."[58] Nor did marriage shield a female from the monster intemperance, as the endless series of beaten, broken, and poverty-stricken wives who inhabit temperance literature bears testimony. These wives were not entirely innocent victims. Some were like the young wife in Arthur's "The Circean Cup," who enticed her groom with a glass of wine.[59] Other female characters were themselves the drunken cause of family tragedy. The alcoholism and opium addiction of Sigourney's Louise Wilson, for example, destroyed the domestic bliss of her husband and cruelly maimed her daughter. Louise Wilson, however, had acquired her intemperate habits while her fiancé meandered through Europe for three long and lonely years.[60] The apprehensions of the young woman in her urgent quest for a husband and marital stability provided many a literary occasion for female intemperance.

The male's most pressing adolescent dilemma, acquiring economic self-sufficiency, also became entangled with liquor's enticements. Sargent and Forrester usually presented the male's quandary in tales of a youth's departure from a rural village in search of adventure or employment. Home-loving temperance writers especially frowned on the adventurous life of the sailor. Going to sea was a self-destructive act of rebellion, which exposed the young man to the intemperate tars and the parasitical tavern keepers who haunted every port. Employment in the city posed the dangers of solitude as well as evil associations. A saloon was the sole place of camaraderie for Franklin Evans, a deracinated clerk in New York

City. T.S. Arthur articulated the temptation of tavern society in *Six Nights with the Washingtonians:* "My master, a book binder, didn't care anything about me, further than to see that my work was done. Of course, I sought my own company and my own pleasures," declared an apprentice who found consolation in the tavern and with it, intemperance. Reformation for the young man in the city was particularly difficult: "I felt very lonely, and was frequently troubled with thoughts of the tavern and my old companions."[61]

Village exiles and poor men's sons, however, were not the only victims of drink. The fictional catalogue of inebriates included young doctors, lawyers, businessmen, and even ministers. The typical arena of temptation for prosperous young professionals was the fashionable social circle. The simple social gesture of accepting a glass of wine brought on the drunken decline of a wealthy doctor in one of Arthur's tales.[62] Members of the legal profession were particularly susceptible to this variety of temptation. Sargent told of one Arthur Middleton, a prosperous lawyer, prominent politician, and champion of the temperance cause. Middleton, however, scoffed at the doctrine of total abstinence, imbibed wine freely, and ultimately became a drunkard. The principle of total abstinence was aimed especially at members of the prosperous classes and young professionals, those more prone to indulge in French wine than cheap whiskey and rum.

Sobriety was especially necessary for young businessmen. The popular temperance lecturer, John R. Gough, observed that intemperance caused ninety-nine out of a hundred business failures.[63] The temperance stories of T.S. Arthur, Lydia Sigourney, and Lucius Sargent were strewn with "broken merchants," business reversals, and bankruptcies. Drink consumed the energy, attention, and efficiency necessary to operate a business, while its inevitable legacy of vice, gambling, speculation, and mercenary companions absorbed every profit. The path of intemperance often paralleled the plummeting fortunes of once respectable and prosperous mercantile families, as drink shattered the security of wealthy parents, confident young wives, and hopeful young businessmen throughout the fiction of this era.

This literature was calculated to explain and assuage the instability and uncertainty that gripped American families in the 1840s. Intemperance became a catch-all cause for failure to meet the exigencies of new social roles and new social organization. At the same time, temperance writings tried to resolve the tensions between the sequestered childhood recommended for America's young and this unpredictable society. Abstention from alcohol, it was suggested, would guarantee job security, social stability, and happy home life, thereby ensuring a sheltered and peaceful adulthood. Temperance would assist mothers, in particular, in guiding their offspring past all the pitfalls of youth.

Yet, in the process, temperance literature also exposed the inadequacy of purely domestic solutions to the problems of youth. The legendary powers of the mother often faltered within the temperance tale. John Gough told of one mother who had to resort to the temperance lecturer as an emissary to a fallen son. A mother's pleas were useless, in this situation: "My mother is a good woman and I respect her, but I don't love her: every particle of affection for her is burnt out of me."[64] This particular woman had forfeited her maternal influence by introducing her son to liquor in the first place; but even the temperate mother was impotent before the seductions of alcohol. Lydia Sigourney did not substantiate her exuberant praises of female influence in her temperance tales. Both she and Fanny Forrester repeatedly described the failure of the agonized pleas of loving mothers and adoring sisters to dissuade a wayward youth from the path of intemperance.

The feminine wiles of the wife also paled before the demonic power of alcohol. One of T.S. Arthur's Washingtonians jubilantly reported that since he had found a wife, he would never be lonely again and, hence, never tempted to imbibe. The experienced reader of temperance tales, however, knew better than to trust this facile reformation. In the *Drunkard's Daughter* and *Franklin Evans,* the wife's affectionate domestic seductions and even her sentimental death failed to reform a wayward husband. On occasion Arthur himself portrayed the powerlessness of the model wife. Another Washingtonian said of his spouse: "She was ever even-tempered, mild, gentle, and affectionate. And though through a long series of years, I neglected her and debased myself she never uttered a reproach, or neglected a duty."[65] The passivity, gentleness, and submissiveness of the ideal woman did not equip her to do battle with demon rum.

The vagaries of the temperance plots even cast doubt on the efficiency of the contemporary model of child-rearing. One truly successful youth, a rarity in the tales of the 1840s, was not the product of a model home. Robert Flemming of *Alderbrook* was taken from poor parents and put out with a middle-aged, old-fashioned couple, who demonstrated little affection, scolded heartily, and occasionally whipped the lively boy. Robert asserted his independence before the age of twenty-one, going off to become a printer's apprentice in the city and ultimately becoming the governor of the state. Scores of intemperate and unsuccessful characters, on the other hand, were the beneficiaries of affectionate nurture. Strong capacities for affection and acute sensitivity to the emotional needs of others proved a double-edged sword outside the parental home. One of Fanny Forrester's "old playmates" was "almost female in his sympathies," another was his mother's "darling." Both fell prey to intemperance when their affectionate attachments and accommodating dispositions were directed outside their family circles toward peers and associates, who lovingly lured them into taverns. Sargent and Sigourney followed other affectionate sons off to college, out to sea, and into the city, where they found solace for homesickness in the bottle.[66]

The most direct statement of the dangers of excessively affectionate child-rearing did not appear until the 1850s, in T.S. Arthur's classic *Ten Nights in a Bar Room*. The youthful hero of this novel, William Hammond, son of a wealthy judge, idol of his gentle mother, charming, handsome, and talented, stood upon the brink of adulthood with all the advantages of education, fortune, and loving parentage.

> Up to the age of sixteen or seventeen, I do not think he had a desire for other companionship than that of his mother. But this, you know, could not last. The boy's maturing thought must go beyond the home and social circle . . . to step forth into this world, where he was soon to be a busy actor and worker, and to step forth alone, next came in the natural order of progress. How his mother trembled with anxiety as she saw him leave her side.[67]

Beyond the family circle William's ready affection and keen sensitivity, his childhood virtues, became social liabilities. Although these traits won him many friends, toward whom the ever-affable William was compliant and warm, his indiscriminate friendliness tied him to inebriates and gamblers, and chained him to drunkenness. Arthur's portrayal of adolescent susceptibility to drink touched a sensitive nerve in the anxious mind of the loving mother.

Lydia Sigourney's tales also poignantly represented maternal anxiety over a loving son's weakness for alcohol. It was Sigourney's own family history, however, that provided the most damning evidence of the dangers of unalloyed mother love. According to Sigourney, she raised her son Andrew in scrupulous conformity to the pronouncements of moral educators. Upon consultation with a phrenologist, she undertook a campaign to reduce Andrew's overdeveloped faculty of "combativeness." She cultivated his "amative" faculty through association with nesting birds, flowers, and poetry, as well as a loving mother and gentle sister. In childhood, Andrew proved very responsive to this treatment. "In his heart" Andrew's mother discovered an "irrepressible desire of being loved." Andrew's childish journal reflected the designs of his sentimental mother. On virtue, he write: "My goodness is but a poor little leaf. Yet I hope it will grow to be a bud, and a flower to bear fruit in heaven." On ambition Andrew confessed: "I am afraid some children love too much to be rich. I am afraid that I myself do." Andrew also had some thoughts about approach of adulthood: "All should be happy when we can have happiness. For when we grow up there will be other things to attend to."[68]

Andrew Sigourney's youth did indeed bring "other things." At boarding school his poetic ways brought the ridicule of his peers. He rebelled against his mother, trained for military service, and embarked on an arduous tour of the West. But Andrew's pampered childhood had not prepared him for strenuous masculine pursuits. His ego shattered, and stricken with tuberculosis, he returned to his mother, to die.

In a book titled *The Faded Hope* Sigourney offered her readers a curious prescription for the anxiety attached to the severance of filial ties. Sigourney did not disguise a certain pleasure at her son's worldly failure. "His soul was humbled" by his failures in the male sphere. "Scarcely without grateful tears could his mother perceive that everything from her hand was accepted with the docility of a child."[69] Sigourney paraded her son's death before the reading public in her familiar maudlin style; having secured a portrait of his corpse, she exclaimed, "Youth forever! He is there! The parting has not changed him."[70] In death there was a certitute almost preferable to the possible results of relinquishing the child to society: rebellion, temptation, and failure. Andrew Sigourney's mother had been reprieved from the crisis of youth.

Grisly revelations of the underside of maternal nurture such as these were lodged in the very heart of the cult of domesticity. Female authors reveled in poetic and fictional enactments of infant and youthful death; a whole field of sentimental literature, the temperance tale, was devoted to reciting the limitations and defeats of the imperial mother. Sentimental deaths, a favorite ritual of the cult of domesticity, pointed to a fundamental flaw in the social theory and family system that the cult worshipped. The stark divisions between home and world, male and female, were not always complementary; they could not always be knit together into a smooth symbiosis. The sons of domesticity had to bridge that gulf in the youthful period of their life cycles, and their passage from home to the world, childhood to adulthood, was not always a successful one. In popular fiction mothers and authors confided to one another the anxieties provoked by this crisis.

Chapter III

BEYOND AND AGAINST DOMESTICITY: REFORM ASSOCIATIONS AND COMMUNAL SOCIETIES IN THE 1830s AND '40s

Temperance literature was more than an expression of domestic anxiety and more than a confidential conversation between mothers and writers conducted in the quiet of their homes. Temperance tales and tracts invited readers to join a reform movement which promised to assist them in reproducing a generation of temperate sons and daughters. Gathered in temperance societies, parents and children might summon the collective strength with which to eradicate intemperance and all its associated domestic ills. The temperance movement took domestic concerns into a public and social forum. The public temperance pledge, the banners and songs of temperance parades, and institutions like the temperance tavern, brought the crisis of the family life–cycle into a comforting social forum. *The Temperance Token* of 1846 could jubilantly proclaim:

> Wives, mothers, sisters ceasing
> to shed their tears of woe
> Our numbers fast increasing
> Strike terror to the foe.[1]

The family of the 1830s and 1840s, although increasingly portrayed as a specialized child-rearing institution, did not in fact stand alone amid the refuse of a broken agrarian community. The temperance societies and a plethora of associations offered assistance to families in the socializing process. These organizations attempted not only to make the world more habitable, but also to bridge the widening gap between family and society. In the 1830s and 40s, in small towns and large cities, east and west, Americans took to the grass-roots, collective, extra-familial organizations to solve critical domestic issues. They joined maternal associations to discuss child care, formed moral reform associations designed to enforce sexual control, and established physiological societies to enhance the health and morals of families. These voluntary societies introduced a distinctive, sometimes discordant note into the ante-bellum chorus of family anxiety and domestic rhetoric. While these reform associations celebrated the sanctity of the private home and invoked the ideal of female influence and the imperial powers of the mother, their activities often contradicted the tenets of the cult of domesticity. After all, they set up institutions of socialization outside the home and invited women and the young into broader avenues of social discourse and power. During this same period another species of reformer posed an even more direct and complete alternative to domesticity. Small but vocal groups of Fourierists, Shakers, and members of the Oneida Community set up model social systems, in which production and reproduction were organized and integrated in such a way as to throw the whole notion of domesticity into question. Both reformers and utopians brought militant and at times rebellious voices to the domestic discourse of the ante-bellum period. No depiction of family ideology would be complete without consideration of this distinctive variation on the theme of domesticity.

The proliferation of voluntary societies during the early nineteenth century was, in itself, an alteration in traditional patterns of social and familial organization. These voluntary associations of individuals, united around a single project or set of beliefs, planted a new social formation amid the traditional organization of the community around the church, government, and household. The first societies were founded for benevolent, religious, and charitable purposes during the Revolutionary era. Their numbers grew rapidly during the early nineteenth century. Until the 1830s, however, these benevolent associations remained respectful of hierarchical notions of social and family order, and even when they breached topics of urgent concern to families, seemed oblivious to the emerging cult of domesticity.

The American Temperance Society, founded in 1826 and renamed the American Temperance Union in 1833, was born of this predomestic and predemocratic *weltanschauung*. Imbued with the principles of its founder, Lyman Beecher, the Society's object was "the diffusion of information, the exertion of a kind of moral influence, and the power of united, and consistent example . . . to end drunkenness." The *Permanent Temperance Documents* published by the Society, were not designed for the average American, but for the "Preacher, Lawyer, Physician, Magistrate, Officer of Governments, Secretary of a Temperance Society, Teacher of Youth, and educated young men throughout the United States." The ministerial elite was reverently courted: "With great respect and affectionate regard to your high and sacred office we address you. . . ." The venerable members of Congress were also recruited into the Society by way of its adjunct, the Congressional Temperance Union, which constantly flirted with legal control of the liquor traffic and federal action to ban alcohol in the army and navy. The preferred method of the American Temperance Society was to curb drunkenness by beneficent example, legal action, and propaganda, all filtered through a social hierarchy by a network of press, agents, and pamphlets.[2]

Drunkards and the lower orders of society in general, appeared in the *Permanent Temperance Documents* as mere numerals rather than as objects of sympathy; they were submerged in statistical measures of drunkenness, criminality, and pauperism. The family affairs of drunkards appeared not as domestic tragedies but as lurid chronicles of the consequences of excessive drink: "Sometimes wives murdering their husbands, at others, husbands their wives; and worst of all, if worse there can be in such a group of horrors, children murdering their parents." Such gothic family imagery predated sentimental domesticity; it accorded no particular purity to women, nor innocence to children. The American Temperance Society addressed such pronouncements to the patriarchal "heads of households," not to the women or men in the affectionate bonds of the democratic family.[3]

The oncoming tide of domesticity and democracy seeped very slowly into the hierarchical ranks of the American Temperance Union. As early as 1829 the *Permanent Temperance Documents* supplemented hard information with familial sentiments. They proclaimed that liquor "destroys forever the happiness of the domestic circle which is filling the land with women and children in a condition far more deplorable than that of widows and orphans." In 1832 the American Temperance Society mixed principles of reason and affection, resolving to wield "light and love," "sound argument and kind persuasion" in the reform crusade. The female appearing in the earliest documents of the American Temperance Society was pictured in scenes of drunken crime, in pools of blood with a child still clinging to her breast. In the 1840s she was suffused with a domestic halo and pictured gently nurturing principles of temperance in her husband and children. The emerging cult of domesticity had induced even the American Temperance Union to enlist women in their reforming effort.[4]

Through the 1830s the American Temperance Union wavered between democratic domesticity and elitist empiricism in its programs and rhetoric. The society was torn apart by arguments over prevention or reform, and partial or total abstinence. Reform of inebriates and the pledge of total abstinence were both middle-class measures which assumed a sympathy between the respectable reformer and the victim of drink. The Union's ultimate endorsement of total abstinence drove older citizens from the movement, while others rejected moral suasion and democratic self-help, advocating instead legalistic methods of controlling the sale and manufacture of alcoholic beverages. The conflict between systematic hierarchical action and associational uplift so debilitated the American Temperance Union that its fifth annual report pessimistically acknowledged little progress in the cause.[5]

In 1842 the report of the American Temperance Union was suddenly imbued with a new vitality. It exuberantly added up the harvest of redemptions of a "great revival year": five thousand converts in Maine, six thousand in Boston, six thousand in New York City, and many others elsewhere—an estimated fifty to seventy thousand reformed drunkards all told. This escalating conversion rate was phrased in domestic imagery as well as statistics; it brought "relief of domestic misery" and heights "of domestic happiness probably never before realized." One temperance report jubilantly told of a single family where the father and three sons-in-law were all redeemed. The now confident Union reported that reform was usually permanent, reaping "useful husbands, fathers, sons, brothers, and citizens." This avalanche of rehabilitated drunkards and happy families was produced by the explosive reforming method of a group founded by six young Baltimore men in 1840. The reforming method of the Washingtonians infused new life in the lagging movement by convincing the American Temperance Union, bastion of the old hierarchies, to turn its attention to anonymous fathers, sons, and brothers.[6]

The most popular Washingtonian speakers, John R. Gough and H.W. Hawkins, were both young apprentices left unemployed by the depression of 1837. The movement emerged and flourished wherever rootless young wage-earners gathered. Temperance associations served as social intermediaries between uprooted youths and the anonymous cities. According to Arthur, Washingtonians came together after

> sad experience had proven to each one of that little company that alone he could not stand. But together, shoulder to shoulder, hand to hand, and heart to heart, they felt that though the struggle would be hard, they could and they would conquer.[7]

In attempting to conquer the temptor of youth, intemperance, the associations provided a place of refuge midway between the parental family and the impersonal web of society.

The Washingtonians were typical of the reformers of the 1830s and '40s who enthusiastically embraced both democracy and domesticity. They formed associations, gatherings of sympathetic equals, rather than societies that circulated the ideas of an elite. The associationists bound themselves together to achieve a goal, share the power and euphoria of union, and address their peers, the middling sort, in community assemblages. They were linked by common interests and mutual concerns, not by rational lines of responsibility and authority. Temperance men in the Washingtonian era stood "hand in hand, and heart to heart."[8]

Members of reform associations addressed public opinion in a new manner. Rather than compiling statistics and scientific arguments, they reported the personal trials of the unregenerate. Fictional portrayals of the domestic plight of drunkards were the primary method of encouraging identification with, and egalitarian sympathy for, the unreformed. Rather than convincing by rational argument or the power of superior social status, the associationists practiced "moral suasion" and invited changes of the heart. They operated, in other words, on the same principles as maternal nurture.

Yet while the temperance movement waxed popular on the strength of its domestic appeals and imagery, it was like other reform movements, subtly subversive of the old generational bonds of the family. It invited young men and even the "daughters of temperance" to move outside the family, side-step the deference they owed patriarchs be they situated in the family, the church, or the community, and join their peers in a reforming crusade. The assembled body of heterogeneous ages, sexes, and kin relations experimented with social rather than domestic means of inculcating temperate habits and otherwise solving the problems of youth. In sum, the temperance movement of the 1840s and voluntary associations in general cut through the cult of domesticity with a double-edge, subverting generational bonds and usurping family functions, even as they played on domestic anxieties and reveled in domestic images.

The reform associations of the 1830s and '40s could be subversive of the gender as well as the age hierarchies that marked the traditional family. The rise of feminism out of anti-slavery societies is the most familiar and dramatic example of this radical edge of ante-bellum associations. A second, almost as familiar, but more complex example of the convoluted relationship between reform, feminism, and domesticity is the American Female Moral Reform Society. Recent historians of the movement, such as Carroll Smith-Rosenberg and Barbara Berg, have focused on the militant and feminist implications of the movement's rhetoric and programs.[9] Moral reform was clearly a woman-led movement; the 400 local chapters of the American Female Moral Reform Society far outnumbered and predated the male movement for sexual reform, the Seventh-Commandment Society. The vitriol that the female reformers directed toward male seducers and their audacious defense of the fallen female appear to some modern readers as the epitome of militant feminist consciousness. To view the female moral reform movement in this fashion, however, is to violate its historical context. It can better be seen as an epicycle around the emerging cult of domesticity, and not as a direct pathway toward feminism.

The first issues of the American female moral reform organ, the *Advocate of Moral Reform,* printed in the mid-1830s, described a mode of benevolence very similar to that of the American Temperance Union. Its goal was the prevention of prostitution and seduction, not the reform of fallen men and women. Its object was to reach public opinion through the authoritative judgements of community leaders. Like the Bible, and the tract and temperance societies of the 1820s, the Moral Reform Society devised a system of agents, auxiliaries, missionaries, and publications as its mechanism of informing public opinion. Like the American Temperance Society, it was particularly concerned about the daughters of the upper classes, who had to be protected from the licentiousness of the lower orders, as well as from strangers in their own social circles. In the early years of its publication the *Advocate* read like an exposé, warning of seducers in gentlemen's clothing, reporting flagrant incidents of prostitution, and describing the interiors of brothels. These reforming ladies did not, at first, let false delicacy interfere with their duty to alert the public to such sordid crimes. While eschewing novel-reading, the editors of the *Advocate* occasionally embedded their morals in fiction, but not of the sentimental, domestic variety. The first serial that appeared in the *Advocate* in 1836 was the spectacular tale of an innocent maiden, seduced with a promise of marriage, drugged, despoiled, and left to die in childbirth. This story and other early fiction in the *Advocate* were imitations of Susanna Rowson's *Charlotte Temple* (1791), an archaic relic of the eighteenth century.

At the same time, the *Advocate of Moral Reform* opened its pages to the earliest expressions of domesticity. Like temperance, moral reform was propelled forward by concern for American youth and the confrontation of children with society. Female moral reformers set out to "warn all, but especially the young, against the various arts and seductive influences of the licentious." Like temperance writings, female moral reform literature presented the youthful stage of the life cycle in terms of the fragility of generational bonds and the geographical mobility of sons and daughters. Mothers in agricultural regions with stagnating populations were especially prompt to join the cause of moral reform. In the county of Oneida in upstate New York, societies were swiftly formed in Clinton, Augusta, Whitesboro, Sherburne, and Sauquoit, agricultural villages whose supply of unimproved arable land had been exhausted only recently, sending the progeny of the pioneers westward and to the cities in search of employment. Chapters also emerged in the industrial villages of Oriskany Falls and New York Mills, nearby communities where many of these mothers' sons and daughters were transplanted, as well as the commercial center of Utica. Female moral reform was enacted with special urgency wherever "multitudes of youth are collected who need light and instruction on this subject."[10]

Wherever the societies grew up they addressed themselves to the anxiety of mothers. Utica's moral reformers distributed tracts with titles such as "Appeal to Wives, Mothers, and Daughters," and "Mother Will You Read It." One young widowed mother who greedily accepted the latter tract in 1840 proclaimed: "most gladly will I do so for I feel that I need assistance to train my fatherless boys in purity." She, like many others, stated that "the deep anxiety I feel for my children is daily and hourly increasing."[11] The growth of female moral reform clearly fed off the same anxieties about children that helped generate the cult of domesticity itself. The first volleys in the battle to redeem children and youth sounded very similar, whether they were fired by female moral reformers or New England ministers. One minister mounted the pulpit of the *Advocate of Moral Reform,* for example, to admonish "That every parent is held by obligations equally imperative and powerful to guard his child by early instruction and timely warning from unchaste feelings and licentious habits."[12]

When women responded to the appeals of moral reformers they seized an opportunity to pursue their familial responsibilities in a wider social setting. They practiced family functions in extra-domestic spaces—formal meetings, petition campaigns, visiting committees, public trials, and appeals to legislators. In the process, they created conflict and assumed power, enraging community leaders even as they succeeded in imposing their own exacting standards of sexual purity on public opinion. These reforming women clearly found solace, warmth, and pride of gender in the course of their association. The reports of local chapters reveled in a "beloved sisterhood," and the history of female moral reform is resplendent with forceful images of womanhood and facsimiles of feminist consciousness.

The bold words and deeds of female moral reformers should not be construed, however, as an open rebellion against the consignment of women to a retiring domestic sphere. Female moral reformers took to the streets and the association early in the 1830s, before notions of feminine delicacy and absolute purity had become securely installed in popular ideology. Female moral reform, in other words, was more of a pre-domestic than an anti-domestic phenomenon. Accordingly, the cult of domesticity can be discerned slowly growing up and sprouting branches within the movement itself. During the 1830s the lurid exposés gave way to a "Mother's Department" within the pages of the *Advocate of Moral Reform.* By the late 1830s the *Advocate* was more likely to advise its readers to practice maternal nurture than to publicly confront libertines and brothel keepers. As early as 1838, the pages of the *Advocate* presented the quintessence of domestic ideology in an address to mothers:

> You cannot know in this world how deep is the impression which your earnest and affectionate appeals make upon the minds of your sons and daughters, when alone; and they feel as every child must, whose conscience is not seared with a hot iron, that a mother's affection and soul are seemingly bound up in their welfare. A mother's love will accomplish more than anything else except omnipotence.

By the 1840s female moral reformers, just as surely as the editors of ladies' magazines, were on the way to building mothers' empire.[13]

Yet other alternatives were available to Americans during the decades before the Civil War. Scores of utopian communities were established from New England to Oregon, and each took exception in some way or another to the hallowed tenets of the cult of domesticity. Furthermore, by their very nature, these communities denied the central premise of domesticity—that the private family should retreat into an isolated space where it devoted itself to the specialized process of social reproduction.

Three utopian movements, the United Society of Shakers, Oneida Community, and Brook Farm, illustrate the variety of ways in which ante-bellum communities restructured and reintegrated production and reproduction, male and female roles, and private and public spheres. Each of them played out the dialectic of ante-bellum domesticity in its own distinctive and revealing way. The Shaker band arrived in America late in the eighteenth century and was consolidated into a community early in the nineteenth century. They practiced a unique religion, honoring foundress Ann Lee as prophet and female godhead, and espoused an eccentric sexual doctrine, total celibacy. By the 1840s the Shakers had proliferated into more than a dozen communities renowned for their stability and prosperity. John Humphrey Noyes and converts to his perfectionist theology, established Oneida Community in 1842. Oneida endured and prospered until its $600,000 worth of assets were converted to the Oneida corporation in 1880. Noyes' community sheltered its own brand of sexual eccentricity, a system of communal promiscuity called complex marriage. The third variety of utopian community loosely adhering to the doctrine of Charles Fourier, enrolled such notable transcendentalists and intellectuals as Margaret Fuller, George Ripley, and Horace Greeley. These experiments had an ephemeral existence, disappearing within the decade. Brook Farm, the most renowned American Fourierist phalanx, was the least defiant of domesticity; it was little more than a collection of families, abiding by the conventional sexual code.

These communities, like the reform associations, shared a proclivity toward domestic rhetoric. The Shakers dwelt in "families" and addressed one another as "brothers" and "sisters." George Ripley advertised Brook Farm as "God's great family,"[14] and John Humphrey Noyes organized his perfectionist flock "into larger and more permanent HOMES than those established by marriage."[15] Yet each community resisted the isolation of family from society and amalgamated old patriarchal modes of social organization, innovative new family arrangements, and the intrusive tenets of the contemporary domesticity into a distinctive social system.

Although they varied in the time and tempo of development, each type of community summoned the attention of America's population in the 1840s. Rural and agricultural America was particularly responsive to the enticements of community. Noye's perfectionism arose in an archetypal village setting, the community of Putney, Vermont. Noyes' first converts were friends and family members. The Reverend Hubbard Eastman of Putney, who led community opposition to the perfectionists' "systematic licentiousness," attributed Noyes' popularity to the "respectable and somewhat honorable" position of his family in this New England village.[16] Noyes himself never repudiated the social order in which he was raised; in describing Oneida Community he proclaimed, "our family is a village in itself."[17] In moving from Putney to Oneida, New York, in the revivalistic and reforming "burned over district," Noyes entered the heartland of communitarianism, an area that was also the site of Fourierist experiments. The Shakers also followed the frontier recruitment route, from New England to New York to Kentucky. Ultimately, communities of one variety or another shot up as far west as Oregon.[18]

These communities appealed to the inhabitants of rural areas during a time of frontier instability, population movement, and rapid advances in market agriculture. The Wisconsin Phalanx, for example, addressed itself to rather trivial village tensions:

> The four great evils with which the world is afflicted, intoxication, lawsuits, quarreling, and profane swearing are not found here . . . . There is but a very small proportion of the tattling, backbiting, and criticism of character usually found in neighborhoods of many families.[19]

The concern with lawsuits and the Wisconsin Phalanx's nervous preoccupation with debts, land, and crops, illustrate the intra-family insecurity and the inter-family antagonism accompanying newly commercialized agriculture and rampant land speculation. Communitarianism promised abatement of these uncomfortable conditions. Communities situated in rural areas also proved attractive to uprooted, newly urbanized Americans. A young woman writing in the *Lowell Offering* saw the Shaker village as a resting place for the farmer's daughter turned factory girl, who "longed for some retreat . . . free from all anxiety respecting any future portion of time."[20] John Humphrey Noyes was driven to community by the social rootlessness of the farmer's son in a time of agricultural decline. In a proposal for complex marriage, he lingered over his uncertain and amorphous social status, confessing that he had "no profession save that of servant of God," and lamenting the "irregularity and seeming instability" of his situation.[21]

Noyes also exemplified the domestic uncertainty that made community life so attractive to his generation. He wrote his partner in complex marriage, apologizing for his failure to establish a conventional household and recommending communal living as an ideal substitute, "as a 'certain dwelling place' consistent with the duties of domestic life."[22] Noyes' followers often recalled the domestic apprehensions immediately preceeding their conversions: these included reflections about "my domestic concerns," "trouble of mind by reason of bondage to . . . family," "and a father's guilt after accidentally hurting his child."[23] The celibate Shakers, no less than the promiscuous Oneidans, drew strength and recruited members because of the family tensions of the 1830s and '40s. Catharine Sedgwick suggested that the Shakers would make a model school for housewives, and talked of joining them herself in the loneliness of spinsterhood.[24] Both Mother Ann Lee and Mrs. John Humphrey Noyes resorted to the methods of fertility control of the community (celibacy in one case, male continence in the other) after a series of painful childbirths and miscarriages. Theirs was an extreme solution to the widespread need for methods of controlling births. Both these communities offered relief from the domestic and social tensions inherent in the instability of rural America in an era of agricultural innovation and frontier expansion.

Communitarians, and especially the Fourierists, also spoke to the discomforts of urban Americans and those engaged in industrial pursuits. Albert Brisbane regarded the phalanx as a replacement for the isolated households which proliferated in America's industrial cities. Brisbane's *The Social Destiny of Man* is studded with the terminology of newly specialized social organization: "industry," "occupation," "function," "system." While Brisbane accepted an industrial economy, he opposed its domestic manifestations:

> The cabin, the cottage, or the dwelling house of civilization with its monotony, with the daily repetition of its petty and harassing cares, with its antisocial spirit, its absence of emulation, debilitates the energies of the soul and produces apathy and intellectual death.[25]

George Ripley presented Brook Farm as a "tranquil retreat" from the "pressures of our competitive institutions." Situated eight miles from Boston, Brook Farm also offered relief from the "horror of cities."[26] The Shakers, too, won converts among men experienced in urban and industrial affairs. Universalist minister Fayette Mace found in a Shaker settlement a retreat from the fashionable mores of the urban *noveau riche*.[27] Franklin Evans left city politics and working-class reform to join the Shakers.[28]

At the same time, the cosmopolitan Fourierists were not immune to the seductions of the more rough–hewn Shaker communities. Horace Greeley admitted that:

> The fact stares us in the face that while hundreds of banks and factories and thousands of mercantile concerns managed by shrewd strong men have gone into bankruptcy and perished; Shaker communities established more than sixty years ago are thriving and prosperous today.[29]

These communities and reform associations were remarkably inbred. Franklin Evans of the Shakers had been a Loco-Foco, a woman's rights activist, and an editor of the *Workingman's Advocate*. Many Oneidans were once members of the Moral Reform Society and others had toyed with Shaker celibacy. The interchange of membership between Shaker settlements and the Oneida community is evident throughout their publications. The peregrinations of communitarians even brought at least one Shaker to the North American Phalanx, in the process casually vaulting the boundaries between celibacy and free-love. As Greeley commented:

> with a firm religious base, any socialistic scheme may succeed, though vicious in organization and at war with human nature, as I deem Shaker Communism and the antagonistic or 'free-love' community of Perfectionists at Oneida.[30]

Each of these communities also endorsed one popular cliché of their times, that "this is a reading age." Brook Farm, Oneida, and the Shakers littered the countryside with pamphlets, books, and journals. Noyes prefaced one of several Perfectionist magazines with a defense of printing as "a most efficient means . . . for redemption from the snares of worldly wisdom."[31] Horace Greeley's New York *Tribune* and a periodical, the *Harbinger*, energetically propagated Fourierism. Even the eccentric Shakers sent forth many a volume "in response to the often expressed desire of the public."[32] The communitarians assiduously employed their own printing presses in order to reach the vast reading audience of the 1840s.

In the process Brook Farm, Oneida, and the Shakers wrote their own distinctive renditions of domesticity. The Shakers approximated the village model of domesticity, infused with the utilitarian ethic celebrated by the likes of William Alcott. Noyesism selected romantic love as the most crucial element of embryonic domesticity and forged for it a supportive social environment. Brook Farm, born of urban tensions in the rapidly industrializing 1840s, adopted many tenets of domesticity, often with an enthusiasm akin to the contemporary ladies' magazine. Each of these communities came to terms in one way or another with the domestic concerns of their era, with childrearing, romantic and conjugal love, the dilemma of youth, and the sexual division of labor.

Oneida, the Shakers, and Brook Farm all endorsed affectionate child-nurture, but with some critical qualifications. According to Franklin Evans, Shaker children were raised from infancy in a "mild, gentle, and beneficent" manner, devoid of corporal punishment.[33] Oneida agreed also to "discard the practice of scolding and threatening children but rule them by love and instruction."[34] The Shakers and Oneida, however, did not entrust child-rearing to parents, but assigned it to specialized caretakers, operating in separate children's quarters. Noyes acknowledged that "melodramatic scenes" occasionally ensued when children departed from their mothers, but added that "mothers soon learned to value their own freedom and opportunity of education, and the improved condition of their children more than the luxury of sickly maternal tenderness."[35] This breach of maternal love earned the Shakers and Oneidans widespread condemnation. Mary Dyer appealed to the maternal sentiments of the American audience in her campaign against the Shakers, with whom she had once resided. "My heart was full of grief. My dear babies were gone."[36] A Putney woman attacked Noyesism by noting that "some of the female correspondents [to Noyes' newspaper] seem to take special delight in boasting of their contempt of natural affections."[37]

Fourierist principles also condemned excessive mother love. It was an occupation of the idle, according to Brisbane, which the busy, skilled and educated women of the phalanx would reject. Yet, American Fourierists endorsed the basic principles of affectionate nurture, maintaining that community child-rearing would relieve parents entirely of the disciplinary process which marred the sanctity of family love.[38] In practice the American phalanx never repudiated the control of the nuclear family over child care. The *Harbinger* extolled "home" as the "center of joy to all loving parents and children."[39] America's Fourierists also argued that their "larger family" had the resources to educate children within the community, and thus would spare mothers the heartache of sending their offspring away to school. Communities like Brook Farm contrived to expand rather than constrict the range and power of maternal nurture.

These child-rearing arrangements conformed to each community's expectations for their adolescent members. In the Shaker village and at Oneida, a child could be introduced, early in life, to his adult social role. These communities replicated the pre-industrial apprenticeship system in which sons and daughters acquired training

early in life alongside adults in community fields, shops, and kitch-
ens. In the Shaker village, young men and women also were made
acutely aware of an ascending social order and appropriate behavior
toward their elders, their more talented peers, and their immediate
underlings.[40] At Oneida and in the Shaker settlements, where children were prepared for definite roles in an enclosed social system
which they need never abandon, the internal parental controls of
domestic affection were unnecessary.

Fourierist communities also strove to prepare the child for specific social and economic service. The phalanx, as described by
Albert Brisbane, would assign the work roles of modern society
according to the talents and inclinations of the individual. From
infancy on, each child would be exposed to all the specialized tasks
of an industrial economy. Boys and girls would pass from one trade
to another, testing their skills and their comfort in each, until they
finally selected the most satisfying occupation for adult life. Ritual-
ized competition with children a year or so older was designed to
stimulate the full development of a child's talents all along the way.
These complex arrangements promised to cultivate the child's specific capacities, as well as the competitive and efficient traits necessary for adulthood in an industrial community.[41] Yet in actual practice no American phalanx had the resources with which to duplicate
the modern economy, nor did any community endure into a second
generation. Therefore, none put this complicated division of labor
into practice; none solved the problem of humanely preparing youth
for the specialized occupations of industrial society.

These communities also attempted to reduce or obliterate the
marital anxieties of their young members, a persistent problem even
among the celibate Shakers. Hervey Elkins, who arrived at the New
Lebanon community at age fourteen, reported little occupational
anxiety as a Shaker youth. He learned a useful and congenial trade,
and enjoyed the variety in his daily chores. Questions of love and
marriage, however, seeped into his placid Shaker world, disrupting
his tranquility. One of Elkins' peers left the United Society hope-
lessly lovesick for a "celestial being" whose teeth were "white like
ivory set in the roseate statuary of carnation." Elkins himself with-
stood the momentary seductions of female beauty; "the cause of
such hallucination can be attributed to the love and pleasures which
fire the adolescent breast, becoming by slow and imperceptible degrees, weaker in mature age." Elkins found Shaker life isolated,

stable, and satisfying enough to absorb adolescent marital predilec-
tions and romantic fantasies.[42]

The objective of Oneida community was not to suppress the sexual desires of youth, but to conform them to the community pattern,
complex marriage. To John Humphrey Noyes, sexuality was a
quasi-religious form of communication, whose flowering at puberty
constituted a spiritual rebirth.[43] Therefore, he rejected any extended
moratorium on sexual intercourse during adolescence. At the same
time, however, Oneidans did not allow their youthful members
complete sexual freedom. Young men were tutored in love-making
by middle-aged women; young females consorted with older men.
John Humphrey Noyes assigned himself the task of sexually initiat-
ing girls. One of his pupils recorded the salutary consequences of
this procedure. Only in retrospect did she realize "the great transition I had made from volatile girlhood to earnest womanhood . . . .
After I graduated from the trap shop, and God had given me a
child, you weaned me off and sent me forth to take care of
myself."[44] For this daughter of Oneida, economic and sexual apprenticeship apparently proceeded at the same smooth pace, as
Noyes and his system led her past the pitfalls of adolescence. Thus,
Oneida contrived to reduce the sexual and marital tensions of youth
by clear procedures of transition, and sure programs for future life.

Brook Farm adapted a more laissez-faire attitude toward love
and marriage. In the absence of prescribed rules on such matters the
young unmarried women of Brook Farm suffered the familiar adolescent anxieties. The letters of Marianne Dwight from Brook Farm,
for example, read like a modern teenage diary. Miss Dwight gos-
siped of the romances in the community and vented her resentment
when eligible male communitarians announced their engagements to
others. She disguised and suppressed her blighted hopes with such
announcements as "Why do people foolishly marry? I am getting to
think that Fourier is right and in full harmony there will be no
marriage." Marital alliances introduced jealousy and disharmony
into Brook Farm; backbiting and resentment greeted the inter-
community marriage of Charles Dana and Eunice Macdaniel. Soon
thereafter, the little community disbanded and its members dispersed into isolated homes. Marianne Dwight announced her own
marriage with a notable lack of enthusiasm. She vowed to follow the
"path of duty" and provide her fiancé with "the settled home feeling that marriage gives."[45]

American Fourierism never challenged this reliance on marital love as the ultimate social bond. In fact, it celebrated it in tones as vibrant as the most sentimental romance. According to the *Harbinger* the family should originate in "the most delicate and elevated sentiments of the human heart, they are the crown and flower of life—the opening sunlight of youth, the sweet solace and inspiration of maturity and the joy and support of age."[46] The American Fourierists did insist, however, that loving family relations never be exclusive or selfish. They scorned isolated and intense conjugal love as the nutrient of antisocial capitalistic acquisitiveness. "The deeper and truer the man's love for his wife and children the more it urges him into deadly competition with his breathren [sic]." The community tried to annihilate competitive economic incentives and diffuse affection throughout the community. Yet Brook Farm was too accepting of sentimental domesticity to challenge intense conjugal love in itself. Charles Lane noted that at Brook Farm "something in the marriage bond" seemed to "counteract the universal nature of affections."[47] The affections of Brook Farm residents ultimately flowed into exclusive heterosexual channels. Marianne Dwight's romantic rivalries, Charles Dana's marriage, and Nathaniel Hawthorne's devotion to his fiancćee undercut community–wide affections and harmony. Brook Farm communitarianism floundered amid the jealousy, lopsided loyalties, and nuclear boundaries of romantic and conjugal love.

John Humphrey Noyes was determined to counteract this disruptive exclusiveness of marital love. His disciples parroted his attitude when they wrote that complex marriage "enlarges the heart," ends loving "idolatry," and expurgates romantic "exclusiveness."[48] This expansion of love and sexuality was not a repudiation of the romantic tenets of the emerging domesticity. It was, on the contrary, a way of giving romantic love a wider reign. Noyes aimed to enlarge the range of such love and to preserve the intensity and euphoria of its first flowering. "I know that the immortal union of the heart, the ever-lasting honeymoon which alone is worthy to be called marriage, can never be made by a ceremony."[49] Noyes repeatedly claimed that his system encouraged romance and sustained it long beyond the usual "cooling-off" period which followed the conventional marriage. Noyes' method of birth control, male continence, or *coitus reservatus,* also was designed as the guardian of romance. This practice not only limited births, but brought "the highest bliss of sexual fellowship for any length of time without satiety of exhaustion, and thus, married life may become permanently sweeter than courtship, or even the honeymoon."[50]

By suppressing male orgasm, Noyes' favored birth control technique promised not only to nurture romantic love but also to assuage Victorian guilt.

> Ordinary sexual intercourse is a momentary affair, terminating in exhaustion and disgust . . . the exhaustion which follows naturally breeds self-reproach and shame and thus leads to dislike and concealment of the sexual organs.

Male continence, on the other hand,

> Simply proposes the subordination of the flesh to the spirit, teaching men to seek principally the elevated spiritual pleasures of sexual connection, and restricting the more sensual part to its proper occasions.[51]

Male continence was only one step away from Victorian proposals like that of Lewis Hough, that husband and wife should lie together and give affection without "the ultimate embrace."[52] Both Victorians and utopians had devised methods of dealing with another major marital concern of the ante-bellum era, the control of fertility. The Shakers' answer to this problem, sexual abstinence, was an outright rejection of the romantic excesses of the age. In a poetic contemplation of conjugal and romantic love ("celebrated bridal scenes and banquets of bowers") a Shaker girl exclaimed: "Alas! your path of flowers will disappear. E'en now, a thousand thorns are pointed near." The Shaker, she boasted, had "outlived such day dreams of the mind" as eternal love and marital bliss.[53] After leaving the order of Shakers, Hervey Elkins found that celibacy was the lesser of two evils: "poverty, wretchedness, the rigor of parents, and the arrogance of wealth sever, confine, mutilate, and break more hearts than the apparently cold and rigid injunctions of Shakerism."[54]

In forswearing sexual intercourse and conjugal love the Shakers hoped to escape both heartache and the battle of the sexes. They contended that celibacy allowed for casual, cooperative, male-female relations. Pairs of "brothers" and "sisters" met nightly for congenial discourse. The sister was responsible for meeting her appointed brother's domestic needs, making his bed, ordering his room, and mending his clothes. The Shakers, as well as outside observers, described these daily interactions between males and females as polite, friendly, and devoid of the bickering and mutual recriminations of many conventional marriages. Men and women went soberly about their appointed duties, and except for the absence of sexual relations, resembled the model husbands and wives of William Alcott's manuals.

The Shakers also resembled old New England villagers in their allotment of tasks by sex. Shaker men and women were assigned distinctive household tasks. These were performed within the extended family, and were vital to its economic survival. One Shaker spokesman echoed Puritan principles when he maintained that "the province of the male is in the order of nature to provide for his household, so it is the province of the female to set the household in order and dispense the provisions thus provided."[55] The industrious Shaker sister had neither the time nor the incentives to cultivate the gentle feminine virtues required of the modern wife. Community living and detachment from children permitted Shaker women to share more fully in economic production, albeit in sexually segregated shops and fields. Even as the Shakers pioneered in industrial production, mass-producing medicines and seeds for the American market, this agrarian-style division of labor was maintained.

Oneida varied this sexual division of labor only slightly as its economic base shifted to the mass-production of traps, travel-bags, and mopholders. Women were assigned their traditional tasks, the preparation of food, child care, and housekeeping. Yet the community performed these functions more efficiently than individual households, absorbing the labor of only a few females, and only for part of their working day. Therefore, women also worked in shops and manufacturing. The women of Oneida expressed their economic function in their attire; they donned pantaloons, clothing appropriate for work rather than gracing a drawing room. Nonetheless, the romantic enthusiasm of Oneida brought with it some rarefied ideas about womanhood. Noyes occasionally rhapsodized about the "influence of woman," the emotional sensibility and affectionate power that made demands for "woman's rights" quite unnecessary.[56]

American phalansteries, in contradiction of the pronouncements of Fourier, progressively surrendered to the ethereal vision of femi-

ninity to which Noyes paid only lip service. Brisbane endorsed Fourier's contention that the female's sense of inequality and ennui
stemmed from her exclusion from industrial occupations, with the
consequent underdevelopment of her faculties and her economic
dependence on her mate. Brisbane went on to assert, however, that
"delicate" womanhood shrinks from the "present brutality of industry," and that "industry must be ennobled and refined—it must be
elevated to woman."[57] Rather than offering women economically
useful roles, as in the pre-industrial division of labor, American
Fourierists embraced an elevated, specialized, and increasingly fashionable view of female nature. Horace Greeley wrote in the *Harbinger* that the phalanx offered a woman "protection of her feminine nature," which included her peculiarly "delicate intuition" and
"instinctive promptings of the soul." Greeley also singled out marriage and love as preeminently female matters, to be particularly
cherished in the community:

> She shall be free from all external embarrassments, to enter
> into the holiest relation of life, as the heart may dictate; where
> marriage shall be a tie of sentiment between souls and not of
> pecuniary necessity, where its spiritual aspect shall predomi-
> nate over the material.[58]

The *Harbinger* was full of such sentiments, which in synchrony with
the cult of domesticity, removed women from the basic economic
functions of the community and assigned them a realm of domestic
grace.

   Brook Farm also assigned women a social function that smacked
of domestic imperialism. George Ripley claimed that community
would prepare women to:

> stimulate the intellect of man; with her intuitive wisdom, re-
> fined by all the influence of true education, will be perpetual
> refreshment to his spirit; and the purity of her nature fortified
> by the power of a well-developed understanding will guarantee
> the purity of society.[59]

Ripley endorsed a female role familiar to the readers of ladies'
books in the 1840s—the emotional support of working men from
which would emanate an unobtrusive moral and social power. Yet a

utopian community was not the most appropriate arena in which women could play this role. Nathaniel Hawthorne, for one, left Brook Farm for a "little cottage" where his beloved Sophia Peabody might "keep a feeling of coldness and strangeness from creeping over my heart and making me shiver." One woman and an isolated cottage were required for Hawthorne to create "the sense of perfect seclusion" in which he could write.[60]

Yet the religious and secular communities of the 1840s were originally proposed as alternatives to the private family, as social arrangements which would obliterate specialized social roles and conjugal seclusion. The affectionate bonds of domesticity were insufficient to hold extended families together. The successful operation and endurance of these communities required sophisticated social organization as well as familial warmth, a prerequisite which Brook Farm did not adequately supply. Shakers and Noyesites, on the other hand, created viable societies in microcosm. The United Society achieved community cohesion through a well-defined social hierarchy, which Hervey Elkins compared to the military.[61] Each member was fully aware of his or her standing in this hierarchy, which dictated appropriate behavior toward equals, inferiors, and superiors within the ascending scale of junior and senior members, deacons, and "mother-" and "father"-heads. The Shakers inculcated a sense of inequality and authority in their young offspring: "Your reason teaches you of the necessity of rank," and the "duty of submission."[62] Oneida Community eschewed this precise structure of authority: the perfectionists agreed "without any formal scheme or written laws . . . to regard themselves as one family."[63] The Oneida family was bound together by religious fervor and the authoritative theological expostulations of the charismatic Noyes. The intricate regulations and ranking of complex marriage, also overseen by the patriarchal Noyes, gave further stability to Oneida Community.

Both Oneida and the Shakers coupled these systems of authority and hierarchy with social rituals that cemented individual loyalties to the community. The Shaker rituals—nightly meetings, dances, and the confession upon entrance—were mirrored in the social gatherings and personal criticism sessions of Oneida. These routines implanted community consciousness in individual minds. Yet interpersonal conflict was inevitable in such large families. The Shakers' formula for smoothing over cumbersome family relations was to codify and formalize the most trivial activities. Acceptable forms of address, attire, and posture, all emphasized "good breeding" and "politeness." Young Shakers were trained to respect privacy, speak softly, and avoid ridicule and argument; all safeguards calculated to reduce interpersonal conflict. The Shaker rules and guidebooks read like the domestic manuals of New England in the 1830s and '40s, with directives on cleanliness, order, and manners as well as house-keeping and cooking.[64]

Oneida, born of a more domestic age than the United Society of Shakers, adopted its own distinctive methods of adjusting individuals to the community. Infused as it was with the romantic ideals of the new age, Oneida resorted to love as the insurance of community harmony: *"The affections have withdrawn their strength from every attraction without, and gathered within the charmed circle."*[65] Intense but extended affections obliterated antagonism and individualistic aspirations: "The gravitation of hearts is irresistible. One daily intercourse is rapidly condensing life and intensifying the power of love . . . private tastes are all offered upon the altar of universal love."[66] Reflecting the affectionate excitement of the 1840s, Oneidans relied on the raptures of love rather than precise instructions in domesticity to reduce conflict and order their extended family.

American Fourierism was the product of an even more mature stage of domestic and industrial development, one which eschewed repressive hierarchy and religious dogma as modes of achieving social order. According to Fourier's blueprint, the phalanx was to be ordered by a complex system of industrial occupations and an equally complex psychological mechanism of emulation. Communities were expected to achieve cohesion by satisfying individual passions and by securing for each member a fulfilling and variegated role in industrial production. The occupational structure would be supplemented by a series of social rituals, including parades, uniforms, entertainments, and competitions designed to submerge individual aspirations in community service.[67] American Fourierists, however, underplayed these sophisticated organizational aspects of community. Furthermore, no phalanstery ever acquired the capital and engineering acumen to construct the complicated industrial network wherein its members could discover and then practice their individual skills, talents, and tastes.

Consequently, communities like Brook Farm became little more than ephemeral retreats from urban industrial society, enlarged abodes of domesticity. The *Harbinger* endorsed the defensive home functions of "protection, privacy, quiet, and repose." Ultimately, the community served only a specialized domestic function, providing an escape from, not an alternative to, the modern "social machine." Members of the community found themselves "refreshed and invigorated to go forth with renovated energy, into the various uses of life."[68] American Fourierist communities failed to mold domestic units into a society in microcosm, either the hierarchical village of the Shakers, or the extended loving family of Oneida.

Burdened also with domestic values and conventional attitudes toward marriage, these communities soon disappeared. The dirge rang out for American phalansteries before the end of the 1840s. Reporting in 1847, Greeley's New York *Tribune* announced: "Fourierism Reduced to a Forlorn Hope." Three years earlier in the *Dial*, Charles Lane speculated about Brook Farm's chances of survival:

> Is there some secret leaven in the conjugal mixture which declares all other unions to be out of the possible affinities? Is the mixture of male and female so very potent as to hinder universal or even general union?[69]

Brook Farm was born of this conflict, too much a partisan of the emerging cult of domesticity, too entrenched in the ways of the intense nuclear family, ever to survive as a community. In 1870, John Humphrey Noyes performed an autopsy on the ephemeral communities of the 1840s, and attributed their early demise to their failure to understand the first principle of communism—"reconstruction of domestic relations."[70] According to Noyes, intense and exclusive conjugal and filial relations inevitably bred jealousy, monopolies of affections, and sexual tensions which were disruptive of communal harmony.

As Noyes wrote, however, even Oneida was floundering. Noyes' own community, like the Shakers, had reached its zenith well before the Civil War. Moreover, by 1870, even Noyes had come to recognize the divorce between family and society, or "home" and "business."

> The two principles as they exist in the world are not antagonistic. Home is the center from which men go forth to business,

and business is the field from which they go home with the spoil. Home is the charm and stimulus of business, business provides material for the comfort and health of home.

After the Civil War Noyes clearly perceived the symbiotic contrast between home life and industrial society. At the same time he celebrated the persistence of voluntary associations and intentional communities, as "extensions of the free, loving element, that is the charm of home."[71]

Reform associations, like utopian communities, had lost much of their vitality after the 1840s. Frustrated temperance activists increasingly eschewed moral suasion and associational camaraderie resorting to more coercive legislative methods to eliminate the temptations of alcohol. After 1850 temperance reformers relied less on the voluntary brotherhood and more on the power of the state, as symbolized by the Maine law prohibiting the sale of alcoholic beverages. Female moral reformers also shed their voluntary and collectivist garb as well as their militant rhetoric by 1850. Local chapters initially took up the mantle of feminine purity, but then quietly withdrew into the domestic boundaries of maternal nurture. By mid-century the *Advocate of Moral Reform* was hardly distinguishable from a ladies' magazine. After 1850 reformers and utopians were seduced by the cult of domesticity. Advocates of reforms, be they dietary or sexual, turned away from the difficult process of organizing movements or communities and placed their faith in the magical doctrine of woman's moral power. One temperance writer enunciated this trend in 1851:

> We need more and more of the female influence. What can surpass it? What tyranny of evil can stand before it . . . We need it in the nursery, where mothers can imbue the minds of children with temperance principles. We need it in childhood and youth when a mother's example, and a mother's warning and kind monition are like a golden chain. We need it in society, in the social circle and even in the business of life, wherever woman reigns supreme.[72]

The *Advocate of Moral Reform* expressed little alarm when it reported that "many societies once flourishing are now languishing." By then they too were willing to put their trust in motherhood rather than sisterhood and rejoiced that women were "beginning the work of reform where it should begin, the *right* instruction of children."

By 1850 it was clear that reformers and utopians did not pose a real threat or clear alternative to the development of the cult of domesticity. The basic functions of social reproduction, childcare, socialization, acculturation and emotional support, were rarely delegated to voluntary associations or reorganized communally after 1850. Rather, they were contained within families where they were entrusted more to mothers than to patriarchs. No easy historical explanation for this privatization and feminization of social reproduction can be trotted out and arranged in a mechanical sequence of cause and effect. It is tempting to invoke the nigh universal, seemingly ineluctable, responsibility of women for the physical care of infants as the general grounds for the triumph of domestic maternal socialization. Certainly male power in the widening marketplace, as institutionalized in the legal superiority of men and their control of property, also played a role, giving men a head start outside the household, away from the domain of social reproduction. But a more instrumental, immediate, and ideological factor contributed as well. During the period when local, voluntary associations were experimenting with alternatives to the privatization of social reproduction, a national publishing industry was gearing up for a massive onslaught on popular ideology. That cultural industry and the technology of information it commanded quickly intercepted and drowned out the messages of local bands of reformers. This is the subject of the chapters that follow.

Chapter IV

IMPERIAL ISOLATION:
DOMESTIC ADVICE LITERATURE
OF THE 1850s

"The isolated home is the true home; and this necessarily results from the nature of marriage love, for such love is exclusive."[1] In this pithy characterization of the family, Henry C. Wright made clear the advances of domesticity by the 1850s: the family had been reduced ideologically to a sheltered social unit, whose boundaries were defined by love. Wright's mid-century doctrine reflected his own social retrenchment. Before the 1850s, his name was affixed to reports of maternal associations, defenses of female public orators, and articles in Garrison's *Liberator*. In the decade before the American Civil War, however, Wright produced a series of books on conjugal and sexual matters in which he submerged social reform in the propagation of marital happiness. He now contended that once loving marriages multiplied, "the world's huge, expensive, clumsy and most inefficient apparatus of regeneration, might for the most part be put aside."[2] It was Henry C. Wright who coined the term "empire of the mother" and enthroned the domesticated and retiring female as the monarch of American culture and society.

The 1850s saw two icons—the isolated home and the imperial mother—installed at the center of popular discourse. In ideology, at least, it was possible to devise a domestic physics that placed the family in a remote and narrow social space and at the same time put its cloistered female occupant at the helm of an empire. That idol of domesticity came to hegemony trailing many contradictions, not the least of which was the dubious concept of imperial isolation.

The contrived logic of imperial isolation is apparent in the mode of distributing domestic advice in the 1850s. The discursive domestic manuals of the 1830s and '40s gave way to volumes devoted to discrete family concerns: childcare, marital and sexual relations, and domestic architecture. Even William Alcott succumbed to this new family perspective, contributing books devoted to courtship and marriage rather than the rambling family guides he favored in decades past. The constricted themes that dominated the domestic consciousness of the 1850s were often reduced to narrow physiological and materialistic terms, to questions of the biology of male and female, or the architecture of homes. Family themes focused in on couples in bungalows, removed from society and ensconced in the hermetic world of marriage, love, and home.

The narrowed focus of the didactic domestic writers in the 1850s conformed to changes in the audience they addressed. The literature of the 1850s no longer perceived and presented its readers in a state of social flux and geographic movement. Writers seldom paid their respects to sons and daughters poised on the precipice of an ambiguous adulthood, about to range far afield of their parents' social status and physical surroundings. On the contrary, this literature seemed to speak confidently and without qualification or apology to a secure, largely urban, middle-class audience.

The farm family appeared more as an idyll of the past than as a contemporary reality. The upper class was regarded as a negative model of fashionable decadence, the lower orders as aspirants to middle-range, respectable family status. The sense of urgency that marked the family literature a few decades earlier, the strident tone of New England leaders desperately searching for domestic modes of social order, had also quieted down by mid-century. The didactic family literature of the 1850s was addressed to established nuclear families, who apparently required only the technical assistance of domestic authorities to refine their socially useful functions.

The authors of the 1850s did not address the middle-class family in the old-fashioned neighborly and egalitarian fashion. Rather they posed as experts and professionals, offering special skills to an ill-informed public. Writers on medical matters eschewed home remedies: "Popular medical books, or works on domestic medicine are justly held in slight estimation, not only by the medical profression, but by the more sensible portion of the community."[3] The family should always turn to the physician in cases of disease and accident, not rely on its own resources. Likewise, domestic architects scorned amateur builders, only a trained professional architect could ensure the proper construction of abodes of domestic bliss. Catharine

Beecher elevated housewifery to a "profession,"[4] and Elizabeth Peabody translated the "ideal of mother love" into the "science of education."[5] As Americans settled into industrial society in the 1850s, the family's specialized functions were supervised by scientists, professionals, and proliferating institutions of social service: architectural firms, medical offices, and public schools. All these agencies might appear as intruders into isolated homes, or interlopers in woman's private sphere. In fact their actions contravened some of the women's domestic power as their words exposed the peculiar social operations of the mother's empire.

Childcare remained the central concern of didactic family literature through the 1850s, and motherhood continued to be celebrated in effusive images. Henry C. Wright drew the boundaries of a mothers' kingdom; they extended to "the life and happiness of individuals, the love and harmony of families, the propriety and stability of states and kingdoms, and the protection of life, liberty and person." Yet the expansive maternal jurisdiction Wright described did not provide women much range for purposeful, intelligent, and self-directed action. The imperial powers of the mother, according to Wright, made their chief conquest during pregnancy; character development was "more dependent on the influences that bear upon human beings before birth than any influence that can be brought to bear on them afterwards."[6] Wright was not the only writer of the 1850s to take this secluded route to the mother's empire. Self-appointed experts, scientists, physicians, and agencies outside the home increasingly regarded mothers as the passive instruments of larger physiological and social processes.

The old principles of mother love, conscience, and gentle nurture still appeared in the 1850s, but in a new guise. The American publishers of A. Donne's book on the care of infants prefaced this work with praise for Donne's credentials as a scientist and court pediatrician to Louis Phillippe. Donne then proceeded to reject the excesses of mother love. He was "rather in favor" of breast feeding, but not as an "exaggeration of the sentiments and nature of maternal love."[7] Orson Fowler, the popular American phrenologist, maintained that most mothers err in giving their children the breast TOO OFTEN AND IRREGULARLY, or whenever they cry."[8] Thomas Nichols also advised the American mother to regulate her maternal solicitude and put her child on a definite time schedule for feeding.[9]

The mother's loving care of her infant was now checked by the aura of science; mathematical calculations were employed to determine the time and amount of nourishment.

Writers of the 1850s also contended that the solitary mother was incapable of fulfilling all the needs of her growing child. First, children required the companionship of peers. Elizabeth Peabody offered the kindergarten for this purpose. "The isolated home . . . made a flower-vase by maternal love" was all right for babies. By age three, however,

> The indispensable thing now is a sufficient society for children. It is only in the society of equals that the social instincts can be qualified and come into equilibrium with the instincts of self-preservation.[10]

The sponsors of kindergartens during the 1850s anticipated the twentieth-century rationale for the pre-school; the playful social life of kindergarten would acquaint the child with the wishes of his peers, and nurture adult responsiveness to the needs of co-workers and fellow citizens, not just parents. Elizabeth Peabody still saw the ethical importance of mother love: "The first human intelligence a child expresses is the recognition of that smile."[11] She also continued to inculcate conscience, recommending the use of terms like "serpent" to alert children to the evil appetites within them.[12] In the school, however, the smiles of a playmate, not domestic affection, would reinforce the child's allegiance to conscience. The punishment of the withdrawal of family affection became the withdrawal of kindergarten friendships. Thus, the family's role in moral education was, at the same time, reinforced and diminshed by the preschool of the 1850s.

The function of the school was now clearly perceived as a socializing task. According to Peabody,

> In America, where the excitements of opportunity are literally infinite, the importance of training the speculative mind and immense energy of the people to law, order, beauty, and love (which are all one in the last analysis), is incalculable.[13]

The socialization performed by schools, while similar to domestic education, was more comprehensive. Love became a social princi-

ple, directing individual aspirations into useful and responsible social channels, "law," and "order," as well as "beauty." Furthermore, the model school of the 1850s took greater pains than did the
moral educators of the '30s and '40s to develop the practical skills
necessary for adult social life. Games were scientifically designed to
develop cooperative, democratic relations between children, while
toys were intended to cultivate the skill and workmanlike attention
necessary in industrial society. Childhood play assumed "the serious
form of occupation."[14] Moreover, educators like Mary Mann observed that in American cities nearly "the whole of youth is spent in
schools" and these institutions should be "perfectly independent of
the child's parents" though not in conflict with their wishes.[15] These
schools could introduce American children to a playful facsimile of
adult roles and counteract the insulation of mother love.

Schools and other agencies of socialization also served as a means
of propagating domesticity beyond the middle-class reading audience. Institutional reformers resorted to domestic principles as anti-
dotes to the disruptive potential of the growing class of industrial
workers and the two million immigrants who entered the United
States in the 1850s. As Michael Katz and other historians have
demonstrated, the educational reforms of the period were employed
for this purpose. A spokesman for the upper classes of Beverly,
Massachusetts, for example, viewed public education as a means of
counteracting the domestic non-conformity of the lower orders amid
the "aggregation of large populations in cities and towns always
unfavorable to the physical and moral welfare of our children." In
the face of a family breakdown Horace Mann directed state schools
to "step in and fill the parent's place." Yet the parental arms of the
Massachusetts school system extended only to 20 percent of the
state's children, and these came mostly from middle-class homes.[16]
In fact, the rise of the common school system created an extra-
familial, state-supported, mode of social reproduction on which
middle-class and native-born parents were dependent. In some
ways, the school complemented maternal socializations; in other
ways it competed with domesticity. Either way it encroached upon
the empire of the mother.

Other families, especially those headed by lower-class and immigrant parents, experienced domestic imperialism as direct and coercive state interference. The children of poor and immigrant parents
who were judged juvenile delinquents rather than paragons of moral

education were sentenced to reform schools and houses of refuge. State after state established such institutions during the 1850s, which were often regarded as publicly funded abodes of domesticity, steeped in "those hallowed associations which usually cluster about home."[17] In keeping with current domestic standards, some reform schools employed female custodians, for "these boys many of whom never had a mother's affection, or felt the kindly atmosphere of a woman's love, need the softening and refining influence which only women can give."[18] But the noble ambition of recreating maternal nurture in state institutions soon degenerated into prisons for young domestic deviants, exposing more exceptions and contradictions to the maternal empire.

Economics as well as politics, the market as well as the state, penetrated the domestic sphere of social reproduction during the 1850s for the middle-class as well as the poor. The back of Peabody's *Kindergarten Guide* was given over to more than fifty pages of advertisements for toys, games, and books for children. Enterprising manufacturers had designed a series of thirteen "gifts," each appropriate to the scientific stages of child development. These balls, blocks, modelling clay, and books were sold "in a box, and with a little manual of instruction for mothers, in which the true principles and plans of tending babies so as not to rasp their nerves but amuse without wearying them is very happily suggested."[19] The mother's role in this instance was reduced to following directions from a "little manual." The modern mother had become the supervisor of the play and amusement as well as the moral education of her child.

The children's books of the 1850s suggest that other factors were beginning to subvert the mother's role. Lydia Maria Child's *Flowers for Children* included a poem entitled, "Our Playthings," which listed an impressive array of much loved objects: dolls, ships, wooden animals, china soldiers, and storybooks.[20] The storybooks of the era portrayed girls and boys with insatiable demands for playthings. "The Happy Child," a story by Harriet Beecher Stowe, set out to restrain the excessive appetites of her young readers. Stowe introduced the demanding youngster to a model boy; poor, dying, but content: "see how he seems to enjoy his flowers and his hymn book and his few little playthings."[21] Children's literature such as this .intimated that the American woman's home was being converted into a child-centered world strewn with toys. Even from his transcendental heights, Ralph Waldo Emerson observed that the American child often reigned as "the small despot" of the household.[22]

In literature, if not in life, the child also began to challenge the mother's role as moral educator. Stowe described a boyish hero, "Our Charley," as a "looking glass for grown people, in which they can see certain things become them—in which they might sometimes even see . . . something wiser than all the harsh conflict of life teaches them."[23] Children appeared in literature and educational writings as little cherubs, angelic missionaries who evangelized their homes. The American child took on the literary role of "redeemer," as Bernard Wishey calls it, well before the outbreak of the Civil War.[24] Lydia Child portrayed children as the moral supervisors of many a home, an image of the child that was carried to tens of thousands of American homes by Little Eva of *Uncle Tom's Cabin*. The mere presence of T.S. Arthur's infant "Angel of the Household" reformed a disorderly, impatient mother, and transformed her wayward husband into a prosperous and loving father.[25] One might well ask if such perfect creatures needed to be reared at all.

As if recognizing the validity of this query, literature on child-rearing in the 1850s shifted its concern from childhood education to the procreation of innately virtuous beings. The mother had complete control over her child's moral development not in the nursery, playroom, or school, but in the womb. "Bear in mind, ye mothers of the race, that as you are while bearing every child, so will be that child." If in pregnancy the mother was content, religious, and self-controlled, these traits would be reproduced in her child. She transferred her values to her offspring not by the exercise of her intellect or affections, but via the bloodstream which feeds the fetus, "the grand porter of the whole system."[26]

The physiological determinants of a child's moral birthright could be pushed back even further, beyond pregnancy, to the moment of conception. The character and behavior of both parents at that moment were crucial to the subsequent moral development of the child. Disease, drunkenness, or lust at the time of sexual congress would despoil the angelic nature of the child then conceived. The essential ingredient in salutary procreation was the pure, loving relationship of husband and wife.[27] The formula for breeding generations of healthy and upright Americans was described by Thomas Nichols this way: "The children born in the attraction and passion of a mutual love will be strong and healthy; and thus, freedom will soon give vigor to the race."[28]

Thus, child nurture ultimately became absorbed in the second preoccupation of family literature in the 1850s, marital and sexual relations, steeped in heterosexual love. This was indeed a precarious citadel of empire, wracked by internal contradictions. While the ideal woman of the 1850s fulfilled her most hallowed and imperial role in the act of conception, she was often regarded as so ethereally pure and chaste as to disdain sexual contact. Accordingly, the 1850s literature on domesticity devoted considerable attention and sophistry to sorting out the sexual and emotional relations between husband and wife.

Henry C. Wright contributed another imperial proposition to this discussion by awarding the female the role of arbiter of sexual activity. According to Wright it was the wife who *must decide how often and under what circumstances the husband may enjoy the passional expression of love."* Thomas Nichols put it this way: "It is the part of woman to accept or repulse: to grant or refuse. It is her right to reign a passional queen."[29] Writers on sex anticipated that granting such power to the sex that was often regarded as innately chaste might seriously curtail population growth. To counteract this possibility, they invoked another hallowed female trait—a strong maternal drive. Doctor R.T. Trall, author of a "scientific and popular" treatise on sexual physiology, assured his readers that female control over sex would not lead to the extinction of the species: "Such an objection implies little knowledge of woman," and her "all absorbing, all-controlling" desire to have children.[30] Most writers treated sex as the duty to propagate, rather than an occasion for physical pleasure, a characterization in perfect conformity with the altruistic feminine stereotype.

By assigning control of marital relations to dispassionate women who were determined to become mothers, the writers of the 1850s had contrived, it would seem, an ingenious method of limiting family size without jeopardizing perpetuation of the species. In fact, support for such a sophistry can be extrapolated from the history of American fertility rates. Demographers have recently argued that declining frequency of intercourse was a major cause of the lowered birth rate during the Victorian era.[31]

The physiologists of the 1850s did not deny, however, that the healthy woman was capable of sexual pleasure. The female's clitoris, capable of "the most vivid excitement of pleasure,"[32] could not be easily ignored. In the 1860s Dr. Trall noted that, contrary to widespread belief, the woman's orgasm was not essential to conception, but he still deemed it desirable for healthy procreation. It was actually female sexual desire, lust, rather than the capacity to achieve orgasm, which was either subordinated to the passive, loving faculties of feminine character or denied entirely. Fowler readily admitted that desire for physical intimacy existed in women, but that it rarely took an explicit genital form. Rather, women longed to be chastely fondled, petted, and caressed.[33] Nichols described female sexual arousal as simply a desire to love and be loved. Woman's innocence, love, and maternal instincts became the mainstay of propriety in the 1850s. They would serve to breed angelic children, limit family size, and restrain the heated passions of the male. The pure woman, nonetheless, was to be sexually attractive. According to the phrenologists "SHE IS MOST BEAUTIFUL WHO IS CAPACITATED TO BEAR THE BEST CHILDREN." To attract a male, a female should cultivate a thin waist, large pelvis, and full bust (but by natural means, never by such deceits as padding her breasts). The ideal mate for this gentle, delicate, and submissive maternal beauty was an aggressive, strong, courageous male. Although men were duty-bound to reciprocate women's affections at home, their world of work demanded different character traits: "Woman rules by love, man by force. He breaks the way; she makes that way smooth."[34] These contrasting prescriptions for behavior and personalities were the staples of love for the marital advisors of the 1850s.

The proper contrasts between wife and husband pertained to matters of temperament and biology, not social status or cultural affiliations. Alcott recommended that the married couple be similar in age, property, education, and values.[35] Common backgrounds were an essential feature of the mid-century ideal of conjugal relations, the marriage of companionship. The writers of the 1850s continually berated the husband who spent evenings away from the hearth. One absent husband was reprimanded with the query: "Did he marry for a housekeeper and a mother to his children, or did he seek companionship for life."[36] In a true marriage of companionship the partners' common concerns and interests would commingle around the hearth. At the end of the working day, the world-weary husband required the emotional ministrations of a sympathetic and compatible wife. Henry Wright described such marital harmony as a fulfillment of woman's mission:

> He was alone—a bewildered wanderer in life's escapade—with an ever present call for love and companionship not actualized . . . . From the hour in which our souls were made one, life has been a richer, nobler bloom.[37]

Once again Henry C. Wright had deftly drawn the complicated, apparently paradoxical borders between the isolated home and an imperial domestic system. A lone man in a bewildering society would find completion in the company of a lone but all-loving woman. The latter, by virtue of her boundless love, could cast a warm mantle over the whole, cold, modern world.

Yet even as Wright and his fellow celebrants of companionship, or love-marriage, enunciated this tenet of domesticity, other writers discerned some of its inherent contradictions. Romantic, heterosexual love, the effusive, idiosyncratic, extravagant emotions glorified in these marriage manuals could prove resistant to domestication. Already in the 1850s, domestic experts began to recognize that spontaneous romantic love did not always respect marriage vows, and that its mysterious machinations might even lead to divorce. Before the Civil War this possibility found its way into domestic literature and produced a vociferous debate on the questions of free love and divorce, and in the 1850s assaults on the institution of matrimony were abundant. Thomas Nichols and M. Edgeworth Lazarus, proponents of free love, subscribed to narrow views of marital love. They doubted that romance could flourish in the traditional, legalized state of matrimony. Nichols observed that "at the theater, in the street, everywhere, you can distinguish married people by their indifference to one another."[38] Lazarus attributed novelists' fixation on the period of courtship to their recognition "that in writing for the public they would only make themselves ridiculous by painting love after marriage with the colors of romance."[39] This opposition to the institution of marriage simply put love above the law, a relationship quite appropriate to the celebration of romance by popular writers. Stephen Pearl Andrews expressed the essence of the program of free love in this era:

Indeed, it may be stated as the growing public sentiment of Christendom already that man and woman, who do not LOVE had no right, before God, to live together as MAN and WIFE, no matter how solemn the marriage service which may have been mumbled over them . . . the man and woman who do LOVE can live together in PURITY without any mumbling at all.[40]

Andrews put forth this proposal in an extensive debate with Horace Greeley of the New York *Tribune*. Greeley recognized the root of the subversion of the institution of marriage in the 1850s: "How many have already fallen victims to the sophistry that the ceremony of marriage is of no importance—the *affections* being the essential matter." Greeley excoriated a flourishing "yellow press," which circulated what he called the "free trade sophistry respecting marriage." The former Fourierist saw the family being undermined by individualism, not socialism in the 1850s.[41] Indeed, Stephen Andrews founded his doctrine on the sovereignty of individuals, and Nichols asserted that individuals, not families, were the basis of the state. Free love advocates agreed with most writers on marriage in the 1850s in portraying the conjugal unit as the arena of individual and personal fulfillment as opposed to social activity. Once it was agreed that the home was an exclusive abode of intense affection, "a sanctum where the world has no right to intrude,"[42] individualistic pleas for free love, divorce, and immunity from state interference followed almost inevitably.

The call for relaxed divorce laws was also raised by feminists during the 1850s. At a woman's rights convention in 1860, Elizabeth Cady Stanton presented a rationale for divorce that bore the imprint of the popular view of marriage. "Nothing is sacred in the family and home, but just so far as it is built up and anchored in love." A loveless marriage in Stanton's view, should be quickly dissolved, allowing females to find new objects for their abounding love as soon as possible. Ernestine Ross seconded Stanton's proposal with a now familiar argument: children would be better off in a broken home than in a household infested by the hatred resulting from a bad match. In challenging the indissolubility of a marriage, even feminists betrayed allegiance to a basic tenet of the cult of domesticity, the sanctity of conjugal love in the home and in the heart of the female.[43]

When love proved a too volatile or too feeble means of maintaining the maternal empire, the family experts of the 1850s could turn to a far more palpable, sturdy, and material basis of domesticity, home architecture. Henry C. Wright delineated this third flank of didactic family literature:

> Man needs a home for the body as well as the soul. It is natural and right that a man and woman, living in the conjugal relation, should seek to surround themselves with material beauty and elegance, as well as comfort.[44]

Wright merely sanctioned what was already a feverish domestic and economic activity in the 1850s. Family residences proliferated at a pace rivaling that of the railroad lines of the era, spreading balloon frames across the continent, bungalows through the cities, and cottages out into the suburbs. One pioneering domestic architect, Gervase Wheeler, boasted in 1855 that "the desire to build, to have a home of one's own is implanted in the breast of every American, and I fancy statistics would show that the number of those who own homesteads in this country far exceeds England."[45] Other writers did their best to foster this domestic urge. Orson Fowler advised young husbands to "PROVIDE A HOME FIRST—whatever else you do, or however stringent your poverty."[46]

These enterprising architects of ante–bellum America were not disinterested champions of the home-owning fetish. Their volumes of architectural advice, replete with plans and sketches of model homes, manipulated and capitalized on the prevailing cult of domesticity. These books commonly noted the names, addresses, and rates of urban architectural firms, coupled with warnings against the hazards of amateur home construction. Wheeler, for example, told his readers to put themselves "under the guidance of a professional man," once the decision to build had been made. In the interim, the author "would act as architectural adviser as fully as if his retainer fee had been secured in the shape of a promised five percent."[47] The popular domestic architects of this era surrendered aristocratic principles in order to court a growing middle-class clientele. Andrew Jackson Downing turned, albeit somewhat reluctantly, to designing homes for less affluent Americans, and other architects addressed their manuals to the "capable and industrious man" who needed a "good cheap, commonsense house."[48] These architects courted a mass audience, designing "homes for the million!"

Clusters of homes shot up on the outskirts of American cities, "assemblages of white boxes thrust as near as may be upon the street."[49] The architectural firms did a steady business in "suburban cottages," the ideal rural abodes for all classes escaping the "turmoil of the city." The growth of street railroads permitted the ultimate disassociation of the workplace and family residence, allowing them to be linked by the commuting route of the male breadwinner. For example, by 1860 the fifteen mile radius of Boston was clustered with "railroad villages." The suburban dispersal of Boston's population began in earnest in the 1840s, and by 1850 an estimated 14,000 passengers moved in and out of the city each day on 188 commuter trains. In the following decade the growth of the horse-drawn street railway made suburban travel even more convenient, cheaper, and more popular. A large portion of Boston's middle class fled the inner city by 1855, leaving behind a predominantly foreign-born population. Although commuter fares were still prohibitively high for Boston's working-class families, their dreams of domestic bliss were soon fulfilled. In 1872 Massachusetts law required a "working-man's car" on all commuter lines, and soon after the sons and daughters of immigrants were beating the well-trodden path to "street-car suburbs."[50]

American architects recognized that this escape to suburbia sundered the friendships and neighborly ties of the urban family: "But mark what compensation! You gain a home . . . A HOME! We might leave it there for the world comprehends all that is most prized in life."[51] Proper home architecture, according to its practitioners, facilitated all the functions of the isolated home. Home ownership was, first of all, essential to proper child-rearing. Family-owned homes were not only "nurseries of filial and fraternal affection, but the earliest and best schools of obedience, and duty, of patriotism and piety."[52] Architects also offered their models as ideal settings for the mutual psychological support of husband and wife. Their houseplans fostered repose, comfort, peace, and privacy by "striving to shut out whatever of bitterness or strife may be found in the open highway of the world."[53] Domestic architects of the 1850s enunciated the full-blown ideology of the defensive, isolated home.

> And much of the feverish unrest and want of balance between the desire and fulfillment of life, is calmed and adjusted by the pursuit of tastes, which result in making a little world of the

family home, where truthfulness, beauty, and order have the largest domain.[54]

These architects went on to design homes in compliance with the basic principles of the privatized home. The spacious and rambling rooms where farming families worked, parsons taught, and elites socialized, were superfluous to the new American middle class. Their ideal house plan was a compact cottage, varying primarily in the number of small rooms and degree of ornamentation. Parlors were small, to accomodate family intimacies rather than to cultivate larger social ties. Ideally, each member of the nuclear household was provided with an individual bedchamber for necessary moments of solitude, and to foster strong personal identification with the home spaces. Children especially needed their own bedrooms and playrooms, as well as some say in the overall construction of the house, all in accordance with their new-found centrality in the isolated home. The wife was allotted a kitchen, her "holy of holies." This specialized room was compact, and centrally located, and designed for the convenience of a solitary female worker. The fortunate wife would also be granted terrain for other female functions— a sewing room, boudoir, or perhaps a sitting room. At the pinnacle of bourgeois prosperity, the man of the house could expect a special cloistered portion of the home for a study or library.[55]

As protector of the isolated home, the male was advised to barricade his loved ones from the outside world behind a series of fences, gates, entryways, and locks. Without such devices, he was told, "no residence can be properly regarded as complete."[56] The proper seclusion was difficult to achieve in the apartment houses and tenements of cities: "To possess the best, the true qualifications of a home, each tenement must have its own exclusive grounds, entrance, passages and stairs, as well as individual rooms."[57] Having secured his family a properly isolated and protected nest, the father had fulfilled his major domestic responsibility.

It was now left to the wife to adorn, decorate, and supervise this home. She was proclaimed "mistress of all domestic accomplishments, with ready tact, a quick eye, and a practiced hand to smooth the rough places."[58] Within the protective portals of home, she should amass furnishings and nick-nacks to enhance the interior of the domestic retreat and embellish the exterior of the box-like house with flowers, vines, and shrubbery, sure emblems of domestic

warmth. Male domestic architects, like Downing, politely offered
the lady of the house some advice on these matters.

> Our fair readers will doubtless pardon us for the seeming in-
> trusion on their province, when we say that our object is
> merely to furnish them with reasons for the natural good taste
> which they usually show in this department.[59]

The man's world, industrial society, intruded more upon woman's
sphere than Downing implied. He went on to praise American manufacturers for the tasteful cottage furnishings they were now producing
cheaply and in quantity, and gallantly informed his female readers
where such furnishings might be purchased. Most architects accomo-
dated their readers in this manner, sketching, pricing, and noting the
distributors of domestic paraphernalia such as curtains, porcelain
doorknobs and vases, and labor-saving devices, from stoves to dumb-
waiters. Thus, women were encouraged to become the consumers of
the goods and services of professionals and manufacturers. Woman's
empire was a complex organization, consisting of specialized parts
subject to impersonal market relationships which extended far beyond her own reach or practical control.[60]

Despite the incongruity between the domestic mystique and the
realities of an industrializing society, the cult of the mother's empire
continued to gain converts during the 1850s. Even the fledgling
women's rights movement succumbed to its seductions. This process
is illustrated by the women's rights journal founded by Amelia
Bloomer and titled, ominously, *The Lily*. In its early issues, *The
Lily* printed adamant proposals for sexual equality, and sarcastically
reviewed the "namby pamby sort of articles on women and wives."
By the mid-1850s, however, *The Lily* enthusiastically endorsed a
thoroughly domestic image of woman: "Not in the whole world . . .
is there a character as heroic as the home mother."[61] While she was
to remain in her isolated domestic sphere, the ideal woman was
invested with incomparable power. *The Lily* maintained that:

> Without home, without the domestic relations, the love, the
> cares, the responsibilities which bind men's hearts to the one
> treasury of their precious things, the world would be a chaos,
> without order, or beauty; without patriotism, or social regula-
> tion, without public or private virtue.[62]

Women whose feminism ran deeper than *The Lily*'s also maintained this view. Ernestine Ross assigned to women "a purifying influence" over the crude male world,[63] and Lucretia Mott surmised that women's moral influence might be more productively exercised in the home than in the turmoil of politics.

The idea of woman's moral superiority, inherent in her characterization as pure, loving, and protected from the temptations of the world, ran rampant in the 1850s. Glorifying the female in her home confinement, it precluded a feminist critque of gender asymmetry.

In an 1858 woman's rights convention, Stanton reported that a speech on the "Superiority of Woman" was generally well received, although a few feminists thought that equality of the sexes was quite enough.[65] Even Sarah Grimke, the intransigent feminist of the 1830s, rescinded her demand that men and women be regarded as morally identical. In 1856 Sarah Grimke rejoiced in the "beautiful difference which exists" between the sexes. That difference made women "the great moral power of the world," ensuring the "redemption of the race," defining the "future destiny of mankind." At this juncture, Sarah Grimke felt "no haste, no anxiety to see her sex invested with their rights."[66]

Sarah Grimke and American feminists joined company with a host of celebrants of female moral power and the mothers' empire in the 1850s. Advocates of free love elevated women to the status of "queen and heart of the social circle," the "Social Christ."[67] Horace Mann offered woman dominion over "the empire of Home—the most important of empires, the pivot of all empires and emperors."[68] The poet laureate of domesticity, Lydia Sigourney, told woman that "Her patriotism is to labour in the sanctuary of Home,"[69] and Emerson, the intellectual giant of the age, called woman "the civilizer of mankind."[70] American culture in the 1850s stubbornly reiterated this paradoxical notion of the position of women, confined to isolated bungalows, but simultaneously dictating morality to all mankind. Horace Mann, for example, forbade women to leave home to assume the roles of legislator, politician, or preacher. At the same time, however, he maintained that the female sex could

> open fountains of purity and honor . . . at the fireside, in the village circle, and at the village school, until their influences shall overthrow into the street and the marketplace, and at last reach the hustings and the voting booth.[71]

Yet the immediate village contacts and social duties of women
had been steadily reduced. The ideologues of the mother's empire
eschewed voluntary associations or any activities that diverted
women from the hearth. By 1850 architects admitted that the collections of suburban cottages did not constitute village communities;
cities were regarded as anonymous assemblages of social atoms,
where one's neighbors could not be trusted; and even William Alcott was assailing reform and benevolent associations as "anti-
domestic clubs" which the American woman should scrupulously
avoid.[72] In the absence of intermediary social outlets the moral
power of women was transported in one great, mythical leap from
the fireside circle to the vast expanses of national life, from family
to society, from isolated home to mother's empire.

This female influence spanned the widening breach between the
middle-class home and an increasingly complicated, impersonal society. By the 1850s the social order of the agrarian village was a
distant memory and even the wave of voluntary association had
subsided. In the 1830s, Alexis de Tocqueville had predicted the
outcome of these developments: "The bond of human affection
would become extended but relaxed."[73] He forecast that affectionate loyalties would concentrate in the family, by–pass neighbors and
immediate acquaintances, and attach themselves to distant causes
and intangible ideals such as a national political party, love of country, or the ideal of true womanhood. Sociologists construe these
developments as the advent of a complex industrial society, in which
national ideals and values as well as the institution of the family
serve a vital function of social integration. "Mother's Empire" presented the same social theory as popular ideology. Imperial isolation
was an hyperbole and a contradiction in terms, but it was not a
sociological impossibility. By maintaining a constant vigil in their
detached and individual, sometimes isolated, but rarely unique and
idiosyncratic homes, women could provide the solace to male
workers and the intensive socialization of the young that were indeed vital to social and national order.

The contradiction in the ideal of imperial isolation came not so
much at the level of social theory as in the consciousness of the
individual women who were called upon to manage this domestic
system. No matter how critical their activities were to the operation
of society, they were performed in a narrow and remote social
space. No matter how critical a mother's labor was to the quality of

American life and character, she performed it in isolation from other domestic workers and remote from the formal arena of political and economic power. By virtue of this distance from production and politics, the marketplace and public halls, women experienced a special sense of dependency and alienation. While men might survive and effect change without reproducing themselves, women, the special agents of reproduction, had to rely on their husbands, fathers, and sons, for their basic survival, their political voice, and the justification of their role.

Perhaps the lofty imperial images of the cult of motherhood provided some solace and reassurance in the face of this quandary, but it could not obliterate the real contradictions—the asymmetry, the dependency, and the isolation, which were built into woman's place in the sexual division of labor in the 1850s. To find the most vivid imprint of these contradictions, it is necessary to turn beyond didactic writings to another page of domesticity, and to another chapter.

Chapter V

THE TEARS AND TRIALS
OF DOMESTICITY:
WOMEN'S FICTION IN THE 1850s

By the mid-nineteenth century the American reading public had completed a basic course in domesticity. Legions of readers had advanced from the sober didactic discourses on household order typical of the 1830s to the ornate domestic poetry and parables found in the magazines of the 1840s. Readers of the 1850s had graduated from the extra-familial modes of social reproduction favored by voluntary associations and diligently applied themselves to the expert treatises on sundry family matters. The cult of domesticity had developed a consensus about the functions of the family in an industrial society. The family was a specialized, isolated, child-centered, mother-governed institution, saturated with love. At this juncture domestic discourse could take a new turn, adopt a new tone, speak confidently to its wide and well-educated audience.

In the 1850s domesticity settled down into a new literary form, the novel produced by an increasingly powerful and versatile publishing industry. Firms such as Little, Brown, Appleton, Wiley, Putnam, Ticknor and Fields, and of course, Harpers, pioneered in rationalized, bureaucratic, business organizations. By 1855 the industrial-cultural complex of Harpers, for example, manufactured books on an efficient assembly line, putting forth no less than thirty-five volumes a minute. The book-making process proceeded through seven functionally specialized floors, housing a vast machinery and 300 females to operate its simple levers.[1] *Harper's* magazine proclaimed in 1850:

> Literature has gone in pursuit of the million, penetrated highways and hedges, pressed its way into cottages, factories, omnibuses and railroad cars, and become the most cosmopolitan thing of all.[2]

The arbiters of public taste posted at the nerve center of this cultural industry made a shrewd business calculation when they took to the frenetic publication of fiction in the 1850s. By then the success of magazine serials had undercut the preference of clerics and older citizens for biography, history, theology, and the classics. In the 1820s American publishers printed one hundred and nine works of fiction; by 1840 the output of novels ran to over a thousand titles. A volume of the stories of Sarah Payson Willis sold 180,000 copies in 1853, equivalent to a circulation of one million in the population of 1940.

The reciprocity between popular tastes and publishers' sense of profit was not automatic, however. A syrupy domestic melodrama by an unknown young woman had passed the desks of almost every New York publisher and was about to be rejected by Putnams when a more domestic consciousness, that of George Putnam's mother, happened to sense its worth. Susan Warner's *The Wide Wide World* appeared a year later, swiftly sold 100,000 copies and became a domestic staple. The simple formula employed by Warner, a full-length fictional struggle for domestic bliss against great obstacles, reaped publishing profits for at least thirty years.[3] The literary culture of the 1850s was cosmopolitan in distribution, but domestic in content; the public's tastes and publishers' profit incentives converged in the cult of domesticity. The designation of domestic fiction as the center of popular literary discourse was worked out by trial, error, and accidents; the fortuitous coming together of a major publisher, his mother, and an unknown writer named Susan Warner, exemplifies the process which created domestic culture on a mass national scale in the 1850s.

This rapid and powerful development of domestic literature posed serious problems for women writers. The female writers who molded the first stage of domestic literature, Catharine Sedgwick, Lydia Maria Child, and Lydia Sigourney, found themselves in a confused and alien cultural climate during the 1850s. These New England women began their careers supported by friends, family, and community leaders, not by casting their fate with a nameless public and calculating publishers. Sedgwick left the monetary aspects of her career to her brother; Child and Sigourney personally solicited advice from other community-minded domestic authorities, such as Horace Mann and Timothy Dwight. These women often sent their manuscripts to benevolent associations, tract societies, and Sunday School unions, rather than to publishers for distribution.[4]

When in the 1860s Child wrote her first novel in twenty years, she was not so sanguine about the loss of popularity:

> The book has brought me a great deal of disappointment and humiliation. I did not form any great calculations upon it but I did please myself with the idea that I had five or six friends who would be glad to see that my mind had not lost all its freshness.[5]

The publishing machinery that had taken hold by mid-century perplexed the first generation of literary women. Child reported in 1843:

> I am not invited to write for the popular periodicals of the day for it requires no extraordinary vanity, to suppose that I could write better articles than some who are invited.[6]

Catharine Sedgwick also found American readers to be a fickle audience. In the 1830s she attributed her great popularity to her practical and utilitarian bent, providing "bread stuff . . . suited to the market."[7] By the '50s popular taste had changed, and Sedgwick's confidence had diminished. When in 1857, she, like Child, returned to novel writing after a twenty year lapse, Sedgwick confessed to being "very nervous about my book," even as she eschewed "any foolish expectations about it."[8]

Lydia Sigourney, who had so shrewdly exploited popular domestic anxieties early in the century, still enjoyed substantial literary success in the 1850s and '60s, but her popularity was also waning, and her approach to publishing clearly was becoming outmoded. Her correspondence with Robert Bonner, editor of the New York *Ledger* and a virtuoso cultural capitalist, was defensive, shy, and apologetic. In the 1860s Bonner rejected Sigourney's submissions one after another. In requesting the return of one such poem, entitled, "Seneca Lake," Sigourney revealed her old-fashioned, local, and personal approach to literature: "I suppose it might be the means of gaining several subscribers in this vicinity [Seneca Lake] to the *Ledger*—but you are probably superior to any such consideration, by not choosing to publish it."[9] The piecemeal accumulation of subscribers was not the *modus operandi* of cultural entrepreneurship at mid-century.

Most of the popular women writers of the 1850s were of another generation. They lacked the firm roots in New England communities of their literary predecessors, and had grown up with the cult of domesticity. The most successful novelists of the latter half of the nineteenth century, E. D. E. N. Southworth, Susan Warner, Maria Cummins, Fanny Fern, and Augusta Jane Evans, came from a variety of regions and backgrounds—South and West as well as New England; rich, poor, and nomadic as well as the stable, respectable. They held in common only the status of woman, as conferred by the cult of domesticity within their own lifetimes. The domestic education that the female writers of the 1850s acquired in relative anonymity, mobility, and isolation prepared them to express the most current tensions of modern family life, and reap popularity from an audience of their peers.

In one critical factor, however, these two generations of women were actually quite similar. They all departed from the ideal of domestic womanhood by taking upon themselves the role of family breadwinner. Southworth, like Child and Sigourney before her, could not depend on the financial support of her husband. She took up her pen to support herself and her children after her spouse had abandoned them. Harriet Beecher Stowe and Marion Harland used their royalties to supplement the inadequate salaries of their husbands, both clerics. Unmarried female writers of both generations shared a similar fate; spinster Sedgwick was thrust upon the resources of brothers prone to sickness and economic reversal, while Susan Warner and Augusta Evans saw their royalties evaporate through the poor management of their impecunious fathers. These women were forced to write by the breakdown of one of the most basic principles of the domesticity they celebrated, the model sexual division of labor.

This role breakdown hoisted an awkward burden on the shoulders of female literati. Harriet Beecher Stowe, mother of seven children, wife of a self-pitying and worrying minister, manager of a large and frugal household, as well as a prolific writer, learned to "rejoice for an excuse to lie in bed for I was full tired."[10] Southworth, left to fend for herself, support her children, and wander the continent alone, lamented that she was "broken in spirit, health, and purse—a widow in fate, but not in fact."[11] Lydia Child, struggling to order her household and support her husband's schemes on behalf of the slaves, was heard to groan, "my thoughts have lain buried under a mass of household cares and hourly trials."[12] Sigourney berated herself for failing to balance her domestic responsibilities and literary career: "there must be about me some notorious mismanagement that the claims of literary business and everyday details of the household are so monopolizing and absorbing."[13] Sigourney risked "domestic trouble" to sign her poems against her husband's wishes, and sought on several occasions to separate from him entirely,[14] while Child finally severed her economic partnership with the well-meaning but inept David.

In the face of this precarious balance of gender roles, however, these women writers demonstrated a special craving for male companionship and emotional support. The correspondence of Sigourney, Sedgwick, and Child documents a continuing search for male support and emotional bonds. In middle age both Child and Sigourney engaged in innocent but romantically charged flirtations with younger men.[15] Catharine Sedgwick, who never married, conducted a hectic campaign to acquire dependable objects of affection. In her correspondence she lavished affection on her father, and then on her brothers, whose successive marriages left her bedridden with depression. Sedgwick's diary chronicled an erratic and frustrating emotional history.

> It is difficult to one who began life as I did—the primary object of affection to many—to come by degrees to be first to none—and still to have my love remain in its entire strength and craving such returns as have no substitute.[16]

Sedgwick, like Sigourney and Child, grew up amid dramatic social changes and grew old in the age of industry and domesticity. The flux and uncertainty of their times, the inconsistencies of their gender roles, the disruption of the kinship and social networks that once surrounded them, seemed to breed intense cravings for enduring affectionate bonds. These emotional needs were articulated in the popular literary taste of the 1850s, to which even the likes of Child, Sedgwick, and Sigourney subscribed. Catharine Sedgwick and Lydia Child read the new novels avidly. Child herself was even driven to sentimental composition. Of a tale entitled, "The Quadroon," a sweet, vapid, and obliquely anti–slavery story, Child wrote:

> The young and romantic will like it. It sounds, in sooth, more like a girl of sixteen than a woman of forty and I can give no rational account how I happened to fall into such a strain.[17]

Lydia Sigourney's poetic themes, particularly her treatment of broken–hearted maidens and dying children, also expressed the embryonic sentiments that the popular novelists of the 1850s elaborated to epic dimensions.

It was the literary format in which these two generations of women writers characteristically expressed their domestic needs and anxieties that set the 1830s apart from the 1850s. The younger, more domesticated generation constructed convoluted plots in which reader's romantic expectations were vindicated and her aspirations for love temporarily gratified by the experience of the sentimental heroine who overcame harrowing obstacles to secure a perfect mate and domestic bliss. It was the special genius of the younger generation of popular novelists to provide, in a momentary and imaginary way, the emotional and heterosexual support that even middle-aged and sober women, like Sedgwick, Child, and Sigourney, privately craved. A trip through the literary fare of the 1850s proceeds through endless scenes of severed, strained, failed, and frustrated ties between the sexes. They show, with monotonous uniformity, that heterosexual and marital ties were the nagging problem of domestic discourse in the 1850s.

The domestic discourse proceeded from a set of propositions about the social relations of the sexes, each of which was built into the plot of the typical novel. The most fundamental proposition of domestic fiction was manifest in the gender-typing of the genre itself. This was a literature not only by and for women but one that constrained the imagination and perceived the world within the bounds of woman's sphere. From this basic proposition several others inevitably followed. The first of these is obvious: women must marry if they are to assume central roles in the literature of domesticity. The second was more troublesome: husbands should stand in a position of some superiority over their wives. The third was a compensation for the second: The woman must find some range of power and action within her apparently inferior position.

These three rules of domestic fiction were dealt with in a perfunctory and expeditious manner in the popular novels of the 1850s. Women novelists lost little time in establishing the imperative of matrimony in the lives of their heroines. Loyal to her own spinster status, Catharine Sedgwick did manage to keep the heroine of *Married or Single* from the altar for a lengthy portion of the novel. Yet no sooner had the twenty-three-year-old spinster resolved to "redeem single life from want, from dread and contempt" than a gallant groom appeared to claim her for a "happier fate."[18]

T.S. Arthur, in a work entitled, *Married and Single,* was not at all ambivalent on this issue; he considered it well nigh impossible for a single person to enter the kingdom of heaven.[19] Similarly, no popular writer of the 1850s could dare cast the delicate heroine into the desert of spinsterhood. Even masculine works, such as the adventurous stories of Sylvannus Cobb and the western tales of Emerson Bennett and Charles W. Webber, complied with this literary and cultural convention. Ballroom romances, court intrigues in foreign capitals, and frontier adventures all led to the altar. Although the single state was honored in the noble characters of benevolent spinster aunts, such characters never achieved the status of heroine in the novels of the decade.

Ushering women to the altar was only preparatory to a second and more complicated objective of domestic fiction, constructing the scaffolding of authority and submission that supported every love match. The love scenes of the 1850s ended with something more than kisses. One heroine yielded to her suitor's "superior judgment when in contrarity to her," and found "submission is a pleasure not a cross."[20] Another blue-stocking bride whimpered, "yes sir," when her groom asked, "Do you belong to that tyrant ambition or do you belong to that tyrant Guy Hartwell?"[21] Some ingenious novelists camouflaged female subordination in endearing filial terms. One of Southworth's most dashing heroes recited a loving, "you child! you child!" as he embraced his frail, diminutive bride.[22] Even such beguiling stratagems could not disguise the structural underpinning of happy endings in the 1850s: the union of submissive females with strong authoritative males.

Yet the cult of domesticity had long proclaimed that the gentle female exerted moral authority over her strong mate. The novels were required, therefore, to demonstrate how women readers and characters could achieve moral power from a position of apparent social subordination. T.S. Arthur, in characteristically blunt fashion, offered direct instructions in the wifely art of manipulation. The heroine of Arthur's *"What Can a Woman Do"* tactfully prevented her husband from following his business associates to a tavern: "You are my prisoner, and I will not let you go . . . . And Mrs. Penrose twined her arms around his neck and laid her lips upon his forehead. As she desired it, so it was."[23] Mary Jane Holmes, E.D.E.N. Southworth, Grace Greenwood and Fanny Fern, among others, recounted the reforming powers of conjugal love. Their heroines rejected suitors whose business practices were suspect, and their long-suffering wives reclaimed adulterers, atheists, drunks, and gamblers from moral perdition. The tools of the reforming wife were patience and example. To openly censure, nag, or threaten a wayward husband would only bestir him to further abominations. The feminine principle of power through passivity even operated in the wild West. The fluttering graces of genteel females were cherished even amid the adventure, brutality, and bloodshed of Charles Webber's stories. One of his heroines, "the lightsome, joyous, and genteel" Gabrielle lived among outlaws and Indians and "had humanized them all" by her mere presence.[24]

The pursuit of Texas Rangers and drawing room suitors led the American reading public to the same reaffirmation of model sex roles and ideal marital partnership. The fictional discourse on domesticity did not end here, however. The audience's empathetic involvement with heroes and heroines was elicited by the dramatic, titillating presentation of these values. The novels and serials of the 1850s recorded abortive courtships and bad marriages, threats to this value system, which heightened the exhilaration of the final domestic resolution. T.S. Arthur attributed the fascination with negative examples of domesticity to the monotony of the happy household that experienced "so few incidents to hold the attention strong."[25] The popularity of domestic tragedy also stemmed from genuine fears and problems in the homes of average readers. The broken hearts, spinsterhood, bad marriages, and dying loved ones that were routine in literature were not unknown in everyday life. Yet such commonplace tragedies of family life were not the only domestic troubles highlighted in the fiction of the 1850s. The domestic novel built dynamic plots and dramatic imagery out of the basic contradictions in the domestic ideal itself.

Few of the popular writers of the 1850s directly exposed this underside of domesticity. The critique of domesticity was most often buried in the vagaries of the plot or nuances of tone. Sarah Payson Willis, the ever popular Fanny Fern, was one of the most forthright literary critics of domesticity, and even she clothed her scepticism in humor.

> He wants to be considered the source of your happiness . . . . Your mind never being supposed to be occupied with any other subject than himself, of course a tear is a tacit reproach. Besides you miserable whimperer! what you to cry for? A–I–N–T Y–O–U M–A–R–R–I–E–D? Isn't that the *summum bonum*—the height of female ambition.[26]

Once she unleashed her venom, sweet Fanny Fern was relentless. In her sentimental tales the commanding hero was replaced by the "pusillanious [sic] pussy cat"; "you go plodding through life with him to the dead march of his own leaden thoughts."[27]

Willis was not the only popular author of the 1850s who slyly confessed to some doubts about the cult of domesticity and the character of domestic heroes. In fact, the few male writers who gained a mass readership in the era did so by playing on the contradictions of masculinity. They veiled their criticisms not in humor, but in whimsy. Daniel Mitchell and George Curtis were masters of the genre. They adopted personae who were neither Western heroes nor gallant suitors, but world-weary dreamers. In a wistful ambience far removed from the masculine work-a-day world they constructed fantasies around what were generally considered feminine aspirations. In the immensely popular *Reveries of a Bachelor,* Mitchell's hero yearned for "A Home!—it is the bright, blessed adorable phantom which sits highest on the sunny horizon."[28] The memories and dreams of a homeless bachelor provided an ingenious framework for romanticism, a forum in which many visionary heroines could play out endless melancholy dramas immune to the onset of marital routine and mundane domesticity. Curtis managed to maintain this romanticism within the framework of marriage. His *Prue and I* followed a middle-aged man escaping his tedious job and aging wife in visions of castles in Spain and fantasies of the princesses within.[29] His real life, of course, belied the masculine stereotype of heroism and power. Prue's husband was merely a clerk, a cog in a bureaucratic machine, not a frontiersman or entrepreneur. The popular success of these whimsical discourses suggests that, just as the excessive appetites of the woman for affection were quenched by tales of love and courtship, the burdens of masculine economic responsibility could be relieved in dreams, or dreamy fiction.

Nostalgia, memories of happy youth under the protective parental wing, provided a third mode of expressing the contradictions of domesticity. In *Dream Life,* Mitchell lingered with anguish and remorse over the poignant progress of the adolescent from childhood protection into society. His fondest daydreams were not of conjugal bliss but of his parental home, where the male could rest passively in the warm shelter usually offered only the female in adult domesticity.

> Aye my boy, kiss your mother—kiss her again; fondle your sweet Nelly, pass your little hand through the gray locks of your father; love them while you can. Make your goodnights linger, and make your adieu long and fond, and often repeated. Love with your whole soul—Father, Mother and Sister,—for these loves will die.[30]

Two of the most popular books written by women in the 1850s, Susan Warner's *The Wide Wide World*[31] and Maria Cummin's *The Lamplighter,*[32] also forged a retreat into childhood. Each of these novels followed ingenues in a search not just for a mate but long lost parents as well. In fact, the dominant theme of these very popular tales was the quest for the security of childhood. Both male and female writers turned to literary recapitulations of childhood to escape the tension and contradictions of adult family status. The protective, loving shelter of home seemed most perfect and impregnable under the parental roof.

The literary children of the 1850s, however, were often laden with the anxieties and insecurities of their parents. The childhood created by Warner and Cummins was riddled with the same role confusion and instability as was the fictional presentation of courtship and marriage. The child-hero of Elizabeth Smith's epic, *The Newsboy,* was a ragged waif with the affections of a mother. Struggling to survive alone in the city, Bob, the newboy, managed to collect and harbor a series of orphans poorer and weaker than himself. The intense maternal agonies Bob suffered when one of his foster children died qualified him to speak knowingly to the reading mother:

> I'm glad I has no mother. It's dreadful to make 'em ache-hearted as mothers are. Bob never made anybody weep, and when he dies, the sun will be in the sky and on the face of all just the same.[33]

A childish character like Bob could express the depths of maternal love, and at the same time suggest that such abundance of affection was a dubious blessing, bringing anxiety and emotional vulnerability in its wake. One of Anne Stephens' embittered mothers was also allowed to reveal this underside of mother love: "No mother, well don't mourn for that . . . she won't starve for your sin—or die—die by inches I tell you, because all is of no use."[34]

But above all else the domestic fiction of the 1850s exposed the bitterness that could issue from the relations between adult males and females. These contradictions found yet a fourth mode of literary expression, the explosive plots of the gothic romance.

The most popular work of Anne Stephens' long career, *Fashion and Famine,* brutally exposed the dangers that underlay a woman's emotional dependence on one man. The jaded heroine, Ada Leicester, was deserted by her husband, the only man she ever loved. Ada was left:

> Utterly without objects of attachment; and what desolation is equal to this in a woman's heart? The thwarted affections and warm sympathies of her nature become clamourous for something to love. Her whole being yearned over the blighted affections of other days.

In the despair of unrequited love, Ada Leicaster plotted the ruin of her villainous former mate. Feeling "a knowledge of power over the man who had been her fate," Ada tempted, teased, and ultimately murdered the exploiter of her womanly affections. Anne Stephens had captured the undercurrents of violence in a sex proclaimed passive and weak, but nevertheless infused with the most potent of emotions.[35] Much of the female literature of the 1850s, and particularly the works of Southworth, Evans, and Stephens, disguised this latent animosity in the inadvertent but ubiquitous crippling, killing, or quiet disappearance of the male hero.

The dangerous complications of domesticity were further exposed by a regional variation on the gothic-genre, the Western. Charles Webber's *Tales of the Southern Border* luridly exposed the violence that lurked behind gender stereotypes. The muddled sex roles in his story of a frontier virago named Aunt Beck, for example, provided the makings of domestic homicide. In the course of her frontier life Aunt Beck was at one time or another a bandit, smuggler, and tavern keeper. But she was capable, on occasion, of deep womanly affection. Her first manifestation of femininity was directed towards another sexual aberrant, her sixth son, a delicate creature in a brood of brutal outlaws. When Aunt Beck's husband mocked this pacific boy as feminine and finally murdered him, Beck's maternal instincts catalyzed her masculine responses. Grasping a bowie knife, she stabbed her husband to death, and sent her blood-streaked sons scurrying from the parental household. In the western novel, the rigid concepts of masculinity and femininity gone awry often proved more savage than the much maligned Indians.[36]

Popular writers seldom transcended or even fully comprehended the trials and contradictions of domesticity. In fact, the most insightful critic of ante-bellum domesticity never was awarded popularity by his contemporaries. He was Herman Melville.

In *Moby Dick* Melville relentlessly tested the verities of the nineteenth century, until Captain Ahab sundered the entire moral order as the *Pequod* sank into oblivion. *Moby Dick* by-passed domesticity in search of the ultimate meaning of existence, the deity, the truth, or moral certainty, which seemed to center in the white bulk of the whale. Truth was sought at sea, where neither women nor children dared to go. Starbuck's home-loving values were impotent beside the feverish drives of Ahab, who at the outset threw overboard his pipe, the last remnant of home. Yet at the very time that Melville was writing *Moby Dick* he was composing another moral odyssey, *Pierre,* which was inextricably intertwined with domesticity. By the novel's end the well-bred domestic hero, Pierre, had exhibited the same defiance of conventional morality as Ahab. Pierre's imprecations contained the same fiery metaphors: "I will mold a trumpet of the flames, and with my breath of flame, breathe my defiance."[37] His rebellion was at least as destructive as Ahab's, culminating as it did in the deaths of all his fellow travelers. The ship Pierre wrecked, however, was a domestic vessel, carrying three women—mother, sister, and fiancee—all entangled in the most intense domestic relations. The convention Pierre rejected—marrying a blond, blue-eyed angel according to his mother's wishes and his own romantic inclinations—was also a tenet of domesticity. Yet Pierre's ultimate affront to these values and his consequent self-destruction were also products of his domestic idealism. His tragedy, as created by Melville, was to be caught in the contradictions of the cult of domesticity.

Pierre's transgressions began as an attempt to uphold family virtue. Convinced he had discovered an illegitimate sister in the dark-eyed Isabel, Pierre decided that he could fulfill his brotherly responsibility to her, without dishonoring his father's name or disturbing his mother's peace of mind, only by posing as his sibling's husband. So Pierre left Lucy, his gentle fiancée, "decked in snow white, and pale of cheek. . . . So fair a victim."[38] His heroism actually elevated Lucy to sentimental perfection, purity, and martyrdom. Although carefully contrived to fulfill his responsibilities to the entire panoply of domestic relations, mother, father, sister, and beloved, Pierre's grand gesture was not entirely selfless and sober. Isabel happened to be a very captivating and enticing female: "Womanly beauty and not womanly ugliness, invited him to champion the right."[39] Soon the Victorian hero succumbed as Pierre consummated his false marriage to his alleged sister.

This appalling outcome of Pierre's domestic heroism, apparent incest, stemmed from the Victorian sexual tenets of the cult of domesticity, and the broad and contradictory demands the cult made on males and females. Pierre's relationship to his mother was described as "romantic filial love."[40] When he affectionately addressed his mother as "sister dear," embraced her, kissed her, and playfully adjusted her attire, he conformed to domestic propriety. The self-sacrificing heroine, Lucy, took up residence with Pierre and Isabel posing as a cousin, and assuring her prodigal hero: "Thou art my mother and my brother and all the world."[41] Thus, when Pierre took sister as wife, Melville suggested that there was precedent for incest in Pierre's "fictitiousness in one of the closest domestic relations of life." The "fictitiousness" first seen in Pierre's multifaceted relationship with his mother also had precedence in popular fiction.[42] In the domestic novel, the wife acted as spiritual mother and submissive child, as well as spouse; the husband served as protecting father and asexual brotherly companion, as well as mate; and the isolated conjugal unit subsumed all other social relationships.

Pierre's entire universe was bound up in domestic relationships. His domestic captivity subjected him not only to role confusion, but also to unalloyed female influence. Pierre strove desperately, but unsuccessfully, to construct a masculine model for his guidance and emulation. When his father died, he left the twelve-year-old Pierre "a fond personification of perfect human goodness and virtue." "Not to God had Pierre ever gone in his heart, unless by ascending the steps to that shrine [to his father] and so making it the vestibule of his abstractest religion."[43] Yet this paternal shrine was no more than an idol of oil and canvas embellished with childish memories, merely a musty portrait that symbolized Pierre's moral ambiguity. He did not discover any reliable principles in this blurred and distant image of a masculine family head. On the contrary, in lonely contemplation of his father's portrait, Pierre contrived a resemblance to Isabel, a mistaken perception, which led, in the end, to the deaths of Isabel, Lucy, Pierre, his mother, and his cousin. Pierre finally realized that his kinship with Isabel was the fraud of his young, excitable imagination, stimulated by the melancholy memories of his mother and the romantic nostalgia of his aunt. He floundered in the woman-dominated moral universe of the nineteenth century. Melville's parody of domesticity led to the creation of an American anti-hero. "If physical, practical unreason make the savage which is he? Civilization, Philosophy, Ideal Virtue! behold your victim."[44]

Pierre's conception of Ideal Virtue was culled from domestic literature. The first chapters of the novel and the early years of Pierre's life were a parody of the domestic writings of Melville's contemporaries. Melville satirized the cult of love without mercy:

> Endless is the account of Love. Time and space cannot contain Love's story. All things that are sweet to see, or taste, or feel or hear, all these things were made by Love; and none other things were made by love. Love makes not the Artic [sic] zones but Love is ever reclaiming them.[45]

Heterosexual love, the craving that propelled the plot of the sentimental novel and whetted the appetite of the popular reader, appeared to Herman Melville as a confusion and obfuscation of the organization of gender and family in ante-bellum America. Pierre's agonizing descent into nihilism was provoked by exaggerated expectations of romantic love, by claustrophobic domesticity, and by the moral preeminence of the mother—all the sacred articles in the domestic creed of the 1850s. Moreover, Pierre himself was an aspiring writer who, like Melville, had forfeited popularity by ignoring these literary conventions and the cues of popular domestic discourse. In the person of Pierre, Herman Melville indicted the American writers and publishers who elevated sentimental domesticity to a pervasive national value system.

Most writers of the 1850s recorded only the routine discomforts of love and marriage. T.S. Arthur wrote in *Home Lights and Shadows*, "Oh, how dark the shadows at times, and how faint the sunshine" in the ordinary urban home.[45] In *Married Not Mated* Alice Carey wrote of the endurable but imperfect matches East and West. Grace Greenwood's light offering, *Greenwood Leaves*, recorded the bitter-sweet trials of domestic women:

> It is one of my beliefs that every tolerably pretty maiden (present company excepted) who has arrived at the age of twenty and upwards, has known something like a disappointment of the heart.[47]

Greenwood's "heart histories" chronicled the commonplace anguish of her female acquaintances: unrequited love, deaths of grooms, marital misunderstandings, and, occasionally, a more exotic maladies, such as a groom's arrival at the altar to announce his marriage to the bride's sister.

Countless tears preceded the facile happy ending of a quiet domestic tableau. The most hackneyed and frequent causes of tears—lonely spinsterhood, unrequited heterosexual love, deviant sex roles, childhood nostalgia—fed off fundamental contradictions in the ante-bellum family system, especially its extreme gender asymmetry and the social isolation of the family. The cult of domesticity celebrated a logical and practical impossibility. It bred male and female into dichotomous roles and temperaments, then venerated their union and required their interdependence within an isolated home. The heterosexual tension was lodged at the very center of the domestic mode of social reproduction, and it cast a shadow over the empire of the mother. But it was the genius of this popular culture to inculcate domestic values and then provide, in the novel, an outlet for their expression and catharsis.

The torment of little heartaches and wholesale domestic disasters could not be disguised by a happy ending. They were, in fact, the substance and *raison d'être* of women's fiction in the 1850s. This literary genre did not aspire to some pristine aesthetic standard or to create an imaginary world of abstract beauty, symmetry, and order. Unlike the short family fiction of the 1830s and '40s, the domestic novel was more than an entertaining mode of instruction. The femininized novel of the 1850s was above all else a literary dramatization of the contradictions of the family and the gender system. It titillated readers with repeated images of the fears, annoyances, mundane anxieties, and cataclysmic possibilities of everyday domesticity.

All of this would have been benign enough were it not for the fact that the turgid logic of the cult of domesticity soon burst out of the confines of the novel and found its way into the turbulent center of American politics. Domesticity went on public trial in the 1850s as its tenets became intertwined with the issues of slavery and sectionalism. Popular fiction became a stormy courtroom where authors like Harriet Beecher Stowe argued the domestic merits of slavery, and Southern writers rose to defend the reputation of their families.

Thirty years earlier the discussion of slavery was primarily the prerogative of political and social elites. The intellectual agonies of men like Jefferson and documents like the Declaration of Independence had demolished the moral, political, and philosophical underpinnings for slavery. Yet these arguments were not circulated throughout the population by means of democratic associations or public podiums, much less novels. Several works of literature in the 1820s and '30s addressed themselves to the peculiar institution of the South. But most, like the rambling sketches of Southern life by John Pendleton Kennedy and Caroline Gilman and the stirring novels by Sarah Josepha Hale and Richard Hildreth, eschewed such staples of domestic fiction as romantic love, fragile femininity, and excessive maternal affection.[48] It was the abolitionist polemicists of the 1830s who first invested the question of slavery with domestic sentiments.

When American readers glanced upon the first page of the *Liberator* in the 1830s they found its title nearly eclipsed by the sketch on its masthead; a graphic portrayal of a slave family about to be wrenched apart on the auction block. The verbal as well as the pictorial imagery of the *Liberator* cultivated a personal, domestic response. The poetic salutation in the first issue of the *Liberator* read:

> Art thou a parent? Shall children be
> Rent from thy breast, like branches from the tree
> And damned to servitude, in helplessness,
> On other shores, and thou ask no redress?

The abolitionist movement ingeniously exploited the same family anxieties that fed reform associations and ladies' magazines in the 1830s.

Elizabeth Margaret Chandler utilized this ploy as early as 1829, when she issued her "Appeal to the Ladies of the United States":

> Mother, look down upon that infant slumbering by your side— have not his smiles become as it were a portion of your own existence? . . . Yet were it told to you that just when he was arisen into bold, glad boyhood, when his beautiful bright eyes began to kindle with awakening and early knowledge, when the deep feelings of his heart are beginning to gather them- selves together—and reason and gratitude to mingle with his instinctive love—wert thou told then he should be torn from thee, and born away forever into hopeless, irremediable slav- ery—wouldst thou not rather that death should at once set his cold signet upon him, there where he sleeps in his innocent beauty in the cradle by thy side.[50]

Chandler created a sentimental device that became the mainstay of anti-slavery propaganda. She assumed that the American mother was bound to her child by the most exhaustive expenditure of affec- tion, and that in the course of her gentle nurturing she would merge her own identity with his. When that child reached adolescence and set out on his own, the mother might well fear the breach of mater- nal ties just as her attentive care was bearing fruit. Chandler dis- placed this anxiety onto the slave child. This was the sentimental anti-slavery formula: the conversion of mundane apprehensions of domestic disruption into sympathy for the slave. Elizabeth Chandler, the anti-slavery analogue to Lydia Sigourney, wrote death-bed verse for the *Liberator's* Female Anti-Slavery column.

In the 1830s the potent combination of anti-slavery and domesticity caused widespread public consternation and exploded into anti-abolition riots and impassioned debates about women's proper sphere. In the wake of this controversy both abolitionism and domestic politics became relatively quiescent. It was not until the 1850s that the cult of domesticity became robust enough to sustain a new assault on the family life of the South.

In the two decades before the Civil War, as American editors and publishers unfurled the banners of motherhood and home, Harriet Beecher Stowe was acquiring the skills of domestic sentimentality. Her homiletic tales could be found in magazines from *Godey's* to the *Advocate of Moral Reform*, and were quite indistinguishable from the general run of ladies' magazine material. When her brother, Henry Ward, suggested that her literary abilities be used to forward the cause of the slave, Harriet Beecher Stowe was happy to oblige. The factual and didactic treatments of slavery compiled by the abolitionists of the 1830s, and especially Theodore and Angelina Grimké Weld's *Slavery as It Is*, supplied copious and powerful images of domestic disruption in the slave quarter which she speedily translated into a novel. When *Uncle Tom's Cabin* appeared in 1851 as a serial in the *National Era*, Stowe and the American public were ready, both having completed two decades of domestic education and experience.

Stowe pumped into *Uncle Tom's Cabin* a stream of evocative images drawn from the growing library of domesticity. She managed to weave all the themes of family literature—filial, parental, and conjugal anxieties—into one narrative. Stowe had polished the devices of domestic literature to perfection, painting dying children, anxious parents, and estranged lovers with a poignancy unrivaled in the literature of the period. The richness of detail and breadth of plot in the full-fledged novel allowed for the expression of cherished domestic values as well as innumerable domestic tensions. The anti-slavery novel provided a particularly convenient forum in which to portray familial disaster. In describing the villainous and alien institution to northern white readers, happy endings could be endlessly deferred; the suffering borne by black men and women could be described at length. The domestic disruptions of slave families were both dramatic enough and far enough removed from the experience of white middle-class Northerners to afford these readers an orgiastic domestic catharsis. No wonder, then, that *Uncle Tom's Cabin* became the most popular book of the nineteenth century, selling 300,000 copies in a year. Not even the pro–slavery forces were immune to Stowe's techniques; their novelistic rebuttals gingerly accepted her domestic premises.

By 1852 the American publishing industry had developed the marketing techniques and productive machinery to distribute Stowe's brew of domesticity and anti-slavery sentiments throughout the land. Moreover, not even sectional animosity and the possibility of losing half their customers deterred American publishers from obliging the domestic tastes of their readers. Stowe's proven popularity outweighed omens of disunion, especially since her expressed purposes were conciliatory to North and South. Northern-based publishers, including Harpers and Ticknor and Fields, readily distributed pro-slavery novels of proven domestic worth by Southern women such as Caroline Lee Hentz and Maria McIntosh. These astute purveyors of public taste seemed confident that their sophisticated cultural system could absorb even the volatile issue of slavery.

Both the pro- and anti-slavery novels of the 1850s adopted the sentimental formula and the cult of domesticity wholesale. Each novel set out, first of all, to resolve the romantic difficulties of hero and heroine, and thus establish a home redolent with conjugal love. With white couples this was a simple matter, but infusing black characters with this sentimental notion often proved difficult, for pro- and anti-slavery writers alike. Both Stowe and the Southern apologist J. Thornton Randolph called on mulattoes to play the romantic lead among slaves. These authors also had some difficulty establishing sentimental filial ties among blacks. Again it was usually the mulatto mother who cherished the child in her arms. The mulattoes Charles and Cora of *The Cabin and the Parlor* represented the typical domestic tableau. "Oh! the bliss of that moment when the mother first feels another heart against her own. . . . The sight of Cora and his daughter was like sunshine on his [Charles'] soul."[51]

North and South were also in virtual agreement on their preferred child-rearing techniques. In fact, they often cooperated in rearing model children. The heroine of *The Planter's Northern Bride* was called upon to gently instill discipline in the indulged child of her Southern husband. Aunt Ophelia, Stowe's paradigm of New England virtue, played a similar role in the upbringing of southern children in *Uncle Tom's Cabin*. Pro- and anti-slavery authors also agreed on the angelic nature and redemptive power of such children.[52] The tearful death of little Eva was reenacted at the pathetic deathbed of a planter's son by the slavery apologist, Randolph. Thus, affectionate methods of child-rearing, like romantic love, were values held in common by both the advocates and the enemies of the slave system.

Finally both North and South pledged fictional allegiance to the power and passivity of the mother. The white heroine, North and South, was submissive, meek, and self-sacrificing, armed only with loving smiles and gentle persuasion. These weapons were sufficient, however, to direct husbands along the path to virtue and the correct attitude toward slavery. The coupling of moral power and feminine weakness served as a convenient method of castigating social evil without encouraging overt rebellion. Aunt Phillus, Mary Eastman's pro-slavery answer to Uncle Tom, managed to overpower her shiftless and drunken husband, while she herself was totally compliant before the slave system, submissive to master, mistress, and Christian God.[53] Stowe infused her heroines and, of course, Uncle Tom himself, with such feminine qualities. Eliza shuddered at George's defiance of his master, and discouraged his escape as well as any violent attack on the slave system. In the end, it was only the strength of her maternal instincts and the threat to her child that induced Eliza to brave the escape from slavery.[54]

All the novels of the 1850s upheld social peace and passivity, even while decrying the domestic monstrosities of both the slave system and industrial capitalism. Yet all the popular writers of the day, pro- and anti-slavery, had to expose the fragility of domestic ties and wrench families apart if they were to win the reader's empathy. By ascribing domestic infractions and failures to either North or South, novelists of the 1850s could not help but provoke or exacerbate sectional discord, and in the process transform the moral agency of women into a less benign and pacific influence.

In *Uncle Tom's Cabin* Harriet Beecher Stowe charted the progressive disintegration of Southern family life. In order to create a domestic plot out of the issue of slavery, Stowe had to instill strong family loyalties in the slave population. Thus, the planter's wife,

Mrs. Shelby, was called upon to teach the principal slave characters, Uncle Tom, Chloe, George, and Eliza, "the duties of the family."[55] Yet this was a dubious service, for no sooner had she tied the domestic knot than her husband's economic straits induced him to sell Tom away from his wife Chloe. Tom then proceeded to the next scene of domestic disruption, the St. Claire household, where the corrupting effect of slavery upon the master's family was illustrated: he found a neurotic wife, weak husband, angelic but dying child, and the general disorder of a household operated by slaves. It was on this plantation that young Henrique St. Claire brutally whipped a slave companion, forcing his father to admit that "there is no doubt that our system is a difficult one to raise children under."[56] Even the sentimental *deus ex machina,* the deathbed wishes of the child Eva, could not prevent further domestic disintegration, and Tom proceeded to a third Southern household, the residence of Simon Legree. This was a burlesque of a home; its hearth was employed only to light Legree's cigars and heat his punch, not to warm the domestic circle. Herein was staged the most lurid episode of family disintegration, Legree's lecherous pursuit of both Emmeline, an innocent young girl newly torn from her mother, and Cassy, an embittered woman long deprived of her children. It was here also that Uncle Tom was finally rent from Chloe, by his death at Legree's hands. As Tom had been transported further South and deeper into domestic confusion, George and Eliza, on the other hand, had made their way North through a series of model domestic shelters.

The pro-slavery novels written in the wake of *Uncle Tom's Cabin* accepted Stowe's priorities and values, merely contending that Northern abolitionists were the cause of family disruption in the South, or that slavery provided more domestic security than did the industrial North. Caroline Hentz portrayed the Northern subversion of Southern domesticity in an incendiary guise. She pictured a Northern preacher ingratiating himself to a Southern family only to plot a slave insurrection. "We should like to ask him," she wrote, "if he has no home, no wife or child of his own, no household goods to defend, no domestic penetralia to keep sacred from intrusion."[57] Encouraging slaves to run away was another means by which Northerners reputedly disturbed the South's domestic peace. Hentz recorded the lament of one runaway:

Sometimes it was the voice of Jim saying, "Crissey, Crissey, I told you neber to run away, you'll never see poor Jim no more!" Sometimes they were the voices of little children crying, "Mammy, mammy, arn't you neber coming agin."[58]

By such literary devices the blame for Southern domestic instability was shifted to the North.

Slavery apologists did not hesitate, moreover, to cast aspersions on the domestic life of the North. In *The Lofty and the Lowly,* Maria McIntosh described the family of the wealthy Northern merchant in which domestic values were sacrificed to the ambition of the father and the fashionable aspirations of the wife.[59] The plight of the Northern wage–earner provided even greater sentimental possibilities, and no one exploited them more thoroughly than did J. Thornton Randolph. In *The Cabin and the Parlor,* Horace, the fragile son of a deceased planter, ventured north to win his fortune in order to support his mother and sister. The naive Horace took a position as an office boy, finding to his dismay that his wages never rose even to a subsistence level. As Horace lay on his deathbed crying for his mother, Randolph admonished his Northern readers, "You make slaves of white children, poor orphans, and work them to death. You promise falsely."[60] Randolph also portrayed infanticide as a routine evil of the industrial North and inquired: "What must we think of that system which so brutalizes its victim that it destroys the natural instincts of the mother and makes her think more of a few shillings than of her child."[61] Finally, Randolph noted less spectacular and more prevalent Northern modes of breaking up families.

> The operation of your social system does it continually by compelling families to separate in order that they can live, sending a son to California or the Quinea coast, a daughter West to teach school, or a father to India to die of cholera.[62]

In sum, apologists for slavery fictionally ascribed domestic instability to the North by means of familiar themes: sentimental deaths, brutality, and routine economic exigency.

Such images captured a mass reading audience and even stirred the domestic sensibilities of New England matrons like Lydia Maria Child, Lydia Sigourney and Catharine Sedgwick. Sigourney wrote in the fall of 1860, "my dear friend, I feel so sad-hearted about the clouds in our Southern horizon." Sigourney's sadness blended politics and domesticity. She traced her allegiance to the national union to childhood tales about the patriotism of Washington heard at her father's knee. She appealed to her friends to wield their feminine weapons, prayer and the gentle persuasion of brothers and husbands, to save the beloved Union. Catharine Sedgwick's consciousness of the slavery issue was also enveloped in domestic sentiments. Her interest was aroused by the masculine heroism and feminine values of John Brown, his "high and holy motives," "a beautiful example in this materialistic age."[63] John Brown's raid also sparked the domestic affections of Lydia Child, and rekindled her anti-slavery fervor. She was so touched by John Brown's heroism that she volunteered to be his personal nurse.

The reaction of these women to the slavery debates and sectional conflict of the 1850s illustrates the convergence of domesticity and politics. Sigourney, Sedgwick, and Child not only responded to politics as sensitive and maternal females, but with a strong sense of personal intimacy. In 1860 Lydia Child observed of the popular response to her anti-slavery writings: "More and more, I marvel at the interest people take in personalities. I take almost none in them, except where my affections are concerned."[64] Yet Child's own anti-slavery resurgence was intensely emotional. Her affections became attached to utter strangers like John Brown, just as masses of readers attached their emotions to fictional slave families. Moreover, images such as the dramatic gestures of John Brown, or the matronly grace of Harriet Beecher Stowe helped spread and intensify sectional feelings. When Calvin Stowe reportedly engaged in a polite conversation with the anti-slavery laggard, President Pierce, Lydia Child exclaimed, "If I were his wife, I'd sue for divorce and take it if I couldn't get it by petitioning."[65] This kind of political response not only identified the anti-slavery cause with the actions of a popular literary figure, but also translated politics into a domestic conflict. This melange of politics, popular literature, and family affairs illustrates the centrality of domesticity in the national system of values, and the curious and powerful way mass culture was injected into individual, immediate, "real," experience. Residents of isolated homes attached their personal loyalties and affixed their anxieties to the poignant domestic images and dramas that the American cultural network circulated throughout the nation.

Popular literature did not, however, put forward any viable social or political remedies for the domestic evils it catalogued with such morbid delight. Harriet Beecher Stowe was not an advocate of the immediate abolition of slavery, nor was J. Thornton Randolph plotting the overthrow of the capitalist system. The practical goal of the novelist was primarily to escort heroes and heroines toward a happy ending. The pro-slavery writer strove only to abate the sectional conflict that disturbed the peace of Southern families, and often designed an intersectional marriage alliance for this purpose. Occasionally the novel's resolution incorporated a broader population in the happy domestic finale. The double wedding that concluded McIntosh's *The Lofty and the Lowly* united the Southern hero to a Northern bride and a policy of benevolence toward his slave charges, while his Northern counterpart embraced a Southern wife and plans to build a utopian community for the employees of his factory. Yet such extensions of family responsibility were as rare in fiction as they were in fact in the 1850s. Customarily only the white families and a few trusted house slaves, largely mulattoes, emerged from these novels in full domestic ideality, as custodians of their own nuclear homes.[66]

Once again *Uncle Tom's Cabin* set the formula for this denouement of domesticity. The masculine exertions of George and the maternal loyalties of his wife propelled their escape from the slave system and won them their domestic reward: "A small neat tenement . . . the cheery fire blazes in the hearth; the tea–table covered with a snowy cloth stands prepared for the evening meal."[67] All this testified to Eliza's efficient home management, which enabled George to sit peacefully at his desk while his son was quietly at play. The hero of Stowe's second anti-slavery novel resided at book's end in a similar domestic refuge, a cozy farmhouse, where he reads to his son on a wintry evening. The ideal resolution of the tortuous plots of the slavery novels was simply the establishment of nuclear families, warm fortresses against the confusion and anonymity of the world outside. This resolution was reached, moreover, in the simple manner of a novel's plot, through the individual exertions of heroic characters without any intervening social policies or political decisions.

Writers who, by dint of gender, were steeped in domesticity, discouraged from intellectual exertion, and debarred from practical politics, often proved shoddy social theorists. The domestic argument constricted the oppression of slavery into the narrow vision of sentimental womanhood and contained neither a clear conception of freedom for the black man and woman nor a rational purpose for Civil War. The principle of human freedom stood on a shaky foundation of domestic priorities. *Uncle Tom's Cabin* subscribed to this definition of freedom:

> The right of a man to be a man and not a brute; the right to call the wife of his bosom his wife, to protect her from lawless violence; the right to protect and educate his child; the right to have a home of his own, a character of his own, unsubject to the will of another.[68]

Stowe rendered human rights nearly equivalent to the responsibilities of the model husband; freedom was submerged in domestic conformity. Moreover, this domestic construction of freedom left the female half of the population in the position of protected wife, rather like a child, and similar to the chattels of a benevolent master.

Didactic anti-slavery literature written by males often adopted this same interpretation of freedom. In his tract, "The Family Relation as Affected by Slavery," Charles K. Whipple, relying heavily on the writings of Frederick Law Olmstead and F.W. Higginson, selected slavery's degradation of the popular model of marriage as its greatest evil. This marriage is

> A community of interest not less than of affection. . . . It is the obvious duty as well as the right of a husband to provide for the defense, and security, and comfort, and happiness of his wife, before those of any other human being.[69]

Thus, for a female, the domestic rendition of freedom meant a protected, passive status, rather than control of her own existence. Black men fared no better than women of either race within this ethic. In Whipple's treatise the slave appeared primarily as a racial threat to the white family, a promiscuous example for pure women, a savage companion for angelic children.[70] The rights and dignity of black women and men were repeatedly obscured in the anti-slavery fiction of the 1850s, which abounded in portraits of sambo stereotypes dancing a jig, and favored mulattoes who assimilated the values and assumed the characteristics of white domestic heroes and heroines.

Moreover, the doctrine of domesticity sundered the more inclusive social organizations necessary to uphold human rights and to exercise human freedom. Whipple not only placed conjugal relations above the responsibilities to "any other human being," but also depreciated more extensive social ties. The last section of his tract, devoted to the "Bearing of Slavery on Society at Large," was very brief. Whipple simply stated:

> But is not this question already answered? We have seen the effect of slavery upon the family; and society at large is but an aggregate of families. Doth a fountain send forth at the same time sweet water and bitter?[71]

Whipple parroted the social theory that underlay the cult of domesticity. Individual family units could be relied upon to secure the common welfare and maintain social order. No intermediary institutions, no combination of critical citizens, no collective action by the oppressed, were necessary to ensure social justice.

These families, however, were prey to the values circulated by a centralized, profit-oriented publishing industry. This fountain of domestic values was spewing forth a bitter sectional brew by 1860. Even the gentle voice of Lydia Child rose to a shrill pitch in 1859. In a volume called *The Patriarchal Institution* Child's sentimental sympathy turned to sarcasm as she recommended the benefits of being a slave to her Northern reader: relief from domestic cares and expenses at the auction block, numerous opportunities for promiscuity, and the honor of having the master take your daughter as a mistress. The bitterness and personal immediacy of Child's tone were not likely to encourage sectional reconciliation.[72] It was in this atmosphere of outraged public opinion, with North pitted against South in angry defense of sacred domestic values, that the conflagration of Fort Sumter was ignited.

Surely the Civil War cannot be reduced to a by-product of domestic culture. But neither can it be fully understood without reference to the literary discourse which surrounded it and articulated and interpreted issues of slavery and sectionalism. When the United States came apart at its North-South seam in 1860, the national culture was still weakly woven together by the fragile threads of domestic ideology.

After three decades of sounding the alarm about the breach of

family ties, writers and readers, North and South, had become ac-
customed to the language of domestic disruption and family tension.
Domestic associations, symbols, and evocations had the ideological
power to carry Americans toward Civil War. The most bitter trial of
domesticity was conducted center stage, in the public sphere and on
the battlefields of civil war.

Conclusion

DISMANTLING THE EMPIRE
OF THE MOTHER

The thirty years prior to the Civil War saw a major transformation in the popular ideology of the family and womanhood. This transformation involved fundamental changes in the components of literary culture—in its ideas about the family, the style in which they were presented, the manner and extent of their circulation, and in the tenor of the reader's responses. The development of domestic ideology, beginning in the 1830s with didactic instructions issued by New England elites and culminating in the 1850s with a nationwide binge of novel reading, is something more than a slice of literary history. It chronicles a social and cultural process in which masses of Americans, mostly of the middle social ranks, participated. Readers, writers, and publishers together worked out a set of ideas that interpreted their common experience and arrived at a shared set of values. More than a simple account of these values, popular domestic writing constituted a cult, a ritual incantation recited by a vast congregation composed mostly of women.

The female sex was at the forefront of this critical sequence of changes in nineteenth-century American society, and its story has been written largely by historians of women. In fact, the cult of domesticity has become a center of controversy in the field of women's history. While some scholars perceive ante-bellum domesticity as an ideology that cajoled women into accepting an unequal and constricted position in the home, others contend that, by celebrating the special power and talents of females, the cult granted women a positive gender identity, nurtured collective consciousness, and planted the seeds of feminism. Neither of these interpretations of the relationship between the cult of domesticity and the history of women seems quite appropriate to the ante-bellum era. Both arguments presume that the central axis of discourse about domesticity was drawn between two discreet and antithetical concepts—the family as institution, and woman as individual. The discourse on domesticity between 1830 and 1860 was looser and more rambling than this. It did not focus just on the relationship between women and the family, be it supportive or adversary, but rather on a series of malleable social relationships: those of parents and children, husband and wife, and household and society.

The first of these relationships, that between parent and child, was most critical to the ante-bellum discussion of domesticity. By 1850 the link between the generations was conceived, almost exclusively, as a tight, enduring, and nearly omnipotent maternal knot. Mothers were charged with the responsibility for creating a generation of Americans who conformed to basic standards of middle-class propriety and functioned efficiently and compliantly within a modernizing society. To put it simply, mothers were enrolled in the cult of domesticity as the special agents of childhood socialization. The second domestic relationship, between husband and wife, defined a similar social function. By providing her mate with emotional support and moral guidance, the ideal wife socialized adult males as well as children. The third set of social relationships, which linked isolated households to society at large, was less specific, but equally critical. Under the guise of domesticity woman's private sphere of relations with children and husbands was invested with an expansive social meaning. In the aggregate, the socializing powers of mothers and wives could inculcate social norms, suppress deviant behavior, and maintain social harmony. This third social relationship converted domestic space into an extensive social territory, a kind of moral empire.

Under the banners of the cult of domesticity a whole panoply of social functions was placed under the jurisdiction of women. The domestic labors of females, whether bearing and rearing children, consoling husbands, or feeding, clothing, and evangelizing them both, provided essential social services, cultural coherence, and generational continuity. Many of these domestic tasks, furthermore, had been transferred to women from fathers, parsons, and community leaders. At a time when industrialization and the advance of market agriculture were removing production from the American household, the women of the home were actually accumulating new tasks of social reproduction. To put it another way, the traffic around the American household went in two directions; as production exited, social reproduction entered in its place.

Because the American woman's home was being invested with the critical functions of social reproduction, it is misleading to equate the cult of domesticity with the narrow social space connoted by the term family. The consequences of women's domestic labors were felt far beyond that narrow location, just as their husbands' products and services were transported beyond the work place in a national, capitalist economy. In some ways the term mother's empire symbolizes the extent of women's social jurisdiction during the ante-bellum era better than the word family. The home was only the imperial center, the mother country, from which women launched their vast social influence.

Still, the mystifying effects of the notion of imperial motherhood cannot be ignored. Popular literature exuded the most saccharine and condescending rendition of the feminine mystique. That literature also exposed, however unconsciously, the tensions and contradictions within all the domestic relationships it celebrated.

The relationship of mother and child contained many paradoxes and contradictions. Poetry and prose were replete with images of dead infants and tales of prodigal sons and fallen daughters. The basis of these morbid fantasies is not difficult to locate. Mothers were assigned awesome responsibilities for the next generation, yet their human products were not totally under their control. As a consequence, motherhood was invested with special anxiety and bereft of absolute guarantees of success. Another paradox of the mother-child relationship was inherent in the life-cycle, which ordained that a mother's offspring would eventually leave her side, causing her some measure of pain at the separation. Moreover, in the 1850s the literature on child-rearing began to regard mothering as a natural function, rather than a demanding social duty, and painted children as innately angelic, somehow outside of, and superior to, their mother's tutelage. Accordingly, mothers were robbed of some of the social acclaim and confirmation that their difficult jobs deserved.

The relationship between husband and wife was also rife with tensions and contradictions, easily discernable between the lines of romantic novels. It is not difficult to understand why women readers may have been apprehensive about marrying. Woman's work in life, centered on social reproduction, made her search for a husband especially urgent; she needed a marriage partner not only to father her children, but to provide material support for herself and her offspring. Yet, the female sex was assigned a passive, waiting role in this vital life choice. Women readers may have experienced nightmares of blighted courtships brought on by the fundamental contradictions of gender asymmetry. Women were expected to forge intimate, life-long, interdependent relationships with beings, who, by virtue of gender, were believed to be their temperamental opposites. Again, it was the problems inherent in a specific social relationship, in this case that between husband and wife, and not the abstract distinction between the family and women that preoccupied writers and readers in ante-bellum America.

As domesticity came to maturity in the 1850s the contradictions within the third set of social relations, those between the household and society, were expressed in a particularly virulent form. When domesticity permeated the literature on sectionalism and slavery it demonstrated the explosive implications of the term "imperial isolation." Beginning in the 1830s, woman's sentence to domestic confinement had been accompanied by promises of extensive social influence, embodied in the cliché "The hand that rocks the cradle rules the world." During the zenith of the cult of domesticity the recitation of that cliché became particularly strident, as the social and cultural reality behind it assumed an especially complicated and confusing form.

By the 1850s middle-class mothers had acquired new power and glory as the chief agents of childhood socialization. But at the same time parental power itself had become a less tangible and reliable commodity, based less in external controls (through property, inheritance, joint labor, and vocational training) and more in the mysteries of "conscience" and "gentle nurture." Furthermore, the women who had been assigned the specialized role of socializing children and nurturing breadwinners were removed from the marketplace, the realm of produciton, and the political arena. They were often bereft of first-hand knowledge of the world occupied by their male domestic charges and denied access to the formal centers of public power. This contradictory nature of the mother's imperial power gave a frustrating, phantom-like quality to women'a connection with society outside their private sphere. That frustration found an outlet first in bombastic rhetoric about women's moral superiority, and then in the translation of women's domestic ethics into arguments for and against slavery. In literature like *Uncle Tom's Cabin* domesticity became more than a household word. It proved to be a potent cultural and political force. The social contradictions of mother's empire were voiced even in the White House in 1862, when Abraham Lincoln greeted Harriet Beecher Stowe with the barb, "So you're the little woman who wrote the book that made this big war."

It would be another century before the walls of woman's sphere had been sufficiently battered to allow feminists a relatively unobstructed view of the contradictions of domestic ideology. Only then could they begin in earnest to dismantle the empire of the mother. Yet even during the ante-bellum era, women writers and readers spelled out the difficulties of managing mother's empire. These voices from the nineteenth century still offer a timely warning of the destructive consequences of dividing up the world's work according to gender, and making facile and invidious distinctions between home and society.

REFERENCES

This study was based almost entirely on the analysis of published primary sources. These family manuals, magazines, novels, and tracts numbered in the hundreds and are listed in the footnotes which follow. To supplement these published documents I examined several manuscript collections of the correspondence of popular writers and publishers. These included the holdings of the Schlesinger Library, Radcliffe; the Massachusetts Historical Society; the Boston Public Library; the New York Public Library; and Butler Library, Columbia University. These collections are also cited in the footnotes.

Introduction

1. See for example, Nina Baum, *Woman's Fiction: A Guide to Novels by and About Women in America, 1820–1870* (Ithaca, N.Y., 1978); Nancy Cott, *The Bonds of Womanhood: "Woman's Sphere" in New England, 1780–1835* (New Haven, 1977); Carl Degler, *At Odds: Women and the Family in America from the Revolution to the Present* (New York, 1980); Mary Beth Norton, *Liberty's Daughters: The Revolutionary Experience of American Women, 1750–1800* (Boston, 1980); Kathryn K. Sklar, *Catharine Beecher* (New Haven, 1973); Carroll Smith-Rosenberg, "The Female World of Love and Ritual: Relations Between Women in Nineteenth-Century America," *Signs* 1 (1975): pp. 1–29; Barbara Welter, "The Cult of True Womanhood, 1820–1860," *American Quarterly* 18 (1966): 151–174; Ann Douglas, *The Feminization of American Culture* (New York, 1977).
2. Ibid.
3. Daniel Scott Smith, "Family Limitation, Sexual Control and Domestic Feminism in Victorian America," *Feminist Studies* 1, Nos. 3–4 (1973): 40–57; Paul David and Warren Sanderson, "The Effectiveness of Nineteenth-Century Contraceptive Practices: An Application of Microdemographic Modeling Practices," International Economic History Assocation, *Seventh International Economic History Conference, Edinburgh, 1978* (Edinburgh, 1978), pp. 67–68; James C. Mohr, *Abortion in America: The Origins and Evolution of National Policy, 1800–1900* (New York, 1978); Nancy Osterud and John Fulton, "Family Limitation and Age at Marriage: Fertility Decline in Sturbridge, Massachusetts, 1730–1850," *Population Studies* 30 (November 1976): 481–94; Mary P. Ryan, *Cradle of the Middle Class: The Family in Oneida County, N.Y., 1790–1865* (New York, 1981); Smith, "Family Limitation," pp. 40–57.
4. Susan Porter Benson, "Business Heads and Sympathizing: The Women of the Providence Employment Society," *Journal of Social History* 12 (Winter 1978): 302–313; Barbara Berg, *The Remembered Gate: Origins of American Feminism: The Woman and the City* (New York, 1978); Barbara Epstein, *The Politics of Domesticity:*

Women, Evangelism, and Temperance in Nineteenth-Century America (New York, 1981); Keith Melder, *The Beginnings of Sisterhood: The American Women's Rights Movement 1800–1850* (New York, 1977).

5. Thomas Dublin, *Women at Work: The Transformation of Work and Community in Lowell, Massachusettes, 1826–1860* (New York, 1979).

6. Richard Bernard and Maris Vinovskis, "The Female School Teacher in Ante-Bellum Massachusetts," *Journal of Social History* 10, no. 3 (March 1977): 332–45.

7. Clyde Griffen and Sally Griffen, *Natives and Newcomers: The Ordering of Opportunity in Mid-Nineteenth Century Poughkeepsie* (Cambridge, Mass., 1978).

8. Norton, *Liberty's Daughters*, chap. 9.

9. Ellen DuBois, Mari Jo Buhle, Temma Kaplan, Gerda Lerner, and Carroll Smith-Rosenberg, "Politics and Culture in Women's History, A Symposium," *Feminist Studies* 6, no. 1 (Spring 1980): 26–65.

10. John Mack Faragher, *Women and Men on the Overland Trail* (New Haven, 1979); Douglas, *The Feminization of American Culture.*

11. See Gerda Lerner, *The Majority Finds its Past* (New York, 1980) for an example of this approach.

12. Cott, *Bonds of Womanhood*, pp. 13–14.

13. Degler, *At Odds*, pp. 473–74.

14. Dublin, *Women at Work;* Lawrence Glasgo, "The Life Cycle and Household Cycles of American Ethnic Groups: Irish, German, and Native-Born Whites in Buffalo, New York, 1855," *Journal of Urban History* (May 1975): 339–64; Griffen and Griffen, *Natives and Newcomers;* Paul Johnson, *Shopkeeper's Millennium: Society and Revival in Rochester, New York, 1815–1837* (New York, 1979); Ryan, *Cradle of the Middle Class;* Daniel Walkowitz, *Worker City-Company Town, Iron and Cotton Worker Protest in Troy and Cohoes, New York, 1855–1884* (Urbana, Ill., 1978).

15. Stanley L. Engerman, "The Economic Impact of the Civil War," *The Reinterpretation of American Economic History*, ed. Robert Fogel and Stanley Engerman (New York, 1971), pp. 369–79; Stuart Blumin, "Mobility and Change in Ante-Bellum Philadelphia," *Nineteenth Century Cities* (New Haven, 1969), pp. 198–200; Jeffrey Williamson, "Urbanization in the American Northeast, 1820–1870," *The Reinterpretation of American Economic History*, pp. 426–436.

16. Diane Lindstrom, *Economic Development in the Philadelphia Region, 1810–1850* (New York, 1978); Albert Fishlow, "The Dynamics of Railroad Extension in the West," *Reinterpretation of American Economic History*, pp. 402, 416; William N. Parker, "Productivity Growth in American Grain Farming, An Analysis of its Nineteenth-Century Sources," Ibid, pp. 175–186; Paul David, "The Mechanization of Reaping in the Ante-Bellum Midwest," Ibid, pp. 214–227.

17. Lawrence C. Wroth and Rollo G. Silver, "Book Production and Distribution from American Revolution to the War Between the States," ed. Hellmut Lehman-Haupt, *The Book in America* (New York, 1951), pp. 71, 123; John Tebbell, *A History of Book Publishing in America*, vol. 1 (New York, 1972); Charles A. Madison, *Book Publishing in America* (New York, 1965).

18. Kenneth Lockridge, *Literacy in Colonial New England* (New York, 1974); Albert Fishlow, "Levels of Nineteenth Century Investment in Education," *The Reinterpretation of American Economic History*, pp. 265–73; Monica Kiefer, *American Children Through Their Books* (Philadelphia, 1948).

19. Stephen Thernstrom and Richard Sennett, eds., *Nineteenth-Century Cities* (New Haven, 1969).

20. Ryan, *Cradle of the Middle Class*, chaps. 1–3; Allen Dawley, *Class and Community* (Cambridge, Mass., 1976); Paul Johnson, *A Shopkeeper's Millenium* (New York, 1978).

21. Richard Busacca and Patrick O'Donnell, "The State, Redistribution and the

System of Social Reproduction" (Paper Delivered at the American Political Science Association Meetings, Washington, D.C., 1979).

Chapter 1

1. Henry Barnard, *Memoirs of Teachers, Educators and Promoters and Benefactors of Education* (New York, 1859), p. 266.
2. Ryan, *Cradle of the Middle Class*, chap. 2.
3. Lydia Maria Child, *The Mother's Book* (New York, 1849), p. v.
4. Lydia Maria Child, *The Family Nurse* (Boston, 1837), p. 4.
5. Catharine Sedgwick to Lydia Child, June 12, 1830, Child Papers, Boston Public Library (hereafter BPL).
6. Heman Humphrey, *Domestic Education* (Amherst, 1840), p. 16.
7. "A Dialogue Between a Missionary and a Man and His Wife upon the Duty of Prayer," n.d., Oneida Historical Society, Utica, New York.
8. Horace Bushnell, *Views of Christian Nurture* (Hartford, 1847), p. 207.
9. Humphrey, *Domestic Education*, p. 16.
10. Ibid., p. 22.
11. Theodore Dwight, *The Father's Book* (Springfield, 1834), p. 199.
12. William Andros Alcott, *The Young Husband* (Boston, 1851), p. 57.
13. Lydia Maria Child, *The Frugal Housewife* (London, 1832); Catharine Beecher, *Treatise on Domestic Economy* (New York, 1850); William Andros Alcott, *The Young Housekeeper* (Boston, 1838).
14. Francis Parkes, *Domestic Duties* (New York, 1831), p. 10.
15. William Andros Alcott, *The Young Man's Guide* (Boston, 1833), p. 368.
16. Mrs. N. Sproat, *Family Lectures* (Boston, 1819), pp. 179–84.
17. William Andros Alcott, *The Young Mother* (Boston, 1831), p. 392.
18. Dwight, *The Father's Book*, pp. 105–6.
19. Child, *The Frugal Housewife*, p. 2.
20. Alcott, *The Young Husband*, pp. 23–24.
21. Catharine Maria Sedgwick, *Home* (Boston, 1837), pp. 44–46.
22. Ibid., p. 134.
23. Lydia Maria Child, *Good Wives* (New York, 1849), pp. 55, 267.
24. Child, *Mother's Book*, pp. 161–62.
25. Ibid.
26. Sylvester Graham, *Lectures on Chastity* (Glasgow, 1834), p. 12.
27. William Andros Alcott, *Physiology of Marriage* (Boston, 1855), p. 114.
28. Robert Dale Owen, *Moral Philosophy* (London, 1841).
29. Charles Knowlton, *Fruits of Philosophy* (Chicago, n.d.); Yasukichi Yasuba, *Birth Rates of the White Population of the United States* (Baltimore, 1962), passim.
30. Bushnell, *Christian Nurture*, p. 9; Nehemiah Adams, *The Baptised Child* (Boston, 1836), p. 56.
31. Dwight, *The Father's Book*, pp. 145–46.
32. Sedgwick, *Home*, p. 98; Catharine Sedgwick, *Live and Let Live* (New York, 1837), p. 71.
33. Caroline May, ed., *American Female Poets* (Philadelphia, 1848), p. vi.
34. Ibid., p. 185.
35. Catharine Sedgwick to Theodore Sedgwick, February 1801, Catharine Sedgwick Papers, Massachusetts Historical Society (hereafter Sedgwick Papers).
36. Sedgwick Diary, 1853, pp. 11–112, Sedgwick Papers, MHS.
37. Sedgwick to Kate Minot, September 30, 1849, Sedgwick Papers, MHS.
38. *The Mother's Assistant and Young Lady's Friend*, 1 (October 1841), p. 226.

39. Ibid., 9 (December 1846), p. 121; 9 (July 1846), p. 15.

40. Ibid., 8 (September 1845): 61–69.

41. Frank Luther Mott, *A History of American Magazines* (Cambridge, Mass., 1949), pp. 341–42.

42. *Godey's Lady's Book,* 7 (February 1838), pp. 92–93.

43. Margaret Coxe, *Claims of the Country on American Females* (Columbus, 1842), p. 13.

44. Margaret Graves, *Women in America* (New York, 1855), p. 65.

45. Sigourney, *Letters to Young Ladies,* p. 15.

46. Catharine Beecher, *The Evils Suffered by American Women and Children* (New York, 1846), p. 14.

47. Parkes, *Domestic Duties,* pp. 320–21.

48. William Dewees, *A Treatise on the Diseases of Females* (Philadelphia, 1843), pp. 13–14.

49. Alexander Walker, *Woman Physiologically Considered* (New York, 1843), p. 131.

50. Margaret Fuller Ossoli, *Woman in the Nineteenth Century* (New York, 1869), pp. 103–4.

51. Parkes, *Domestic Duties,* p. 356.

52. *Mother's Assistant,* 9 (July, 1846), pp. 14–15.

53. Ibid. (July, 1847), pp. 10–11.

54. Graves, *Women in America,* p. 60.

55. Sigourney, *Letters to Young Ladies,* p. 12.

56. May, ed., *American Female Poets,* pp. 353–54.

57. Sigourney, *Letters to Young Ladies,* p. 74.

58. Graves, *Women in America,* p. 53.

59. Ibid., p. 60.

60. Timothy Shay Arthur, *The Mother* (Philadelphia, 1845), preface.

61. Coxe, *Claims of the Country,* p. 21.

62. Sarah Josepha Hale, *Housekeeping and Keeping House* (New York, 1845).

63. Coxe, *Claims of the Country,* p. 13.

64. Graves, *Women in America,* p. 142.

65. Andrew Jackson Downing, *Cottage Residences* (New York, 1842), passim.

66. Graves, *Women in America,* p. xv.

67. Beecher, *The Duty of American Women to Their Country* (New York, 1845), p. 1.

68. Coxe, *Claims of the Country,* p. 7; Graves, *Women in America,* p. xv; Coxe, *Claims of the Country,* p. 210.

69. Phillip Greven, *Four Generations: Population, Land and Family in Colonial Andover, Massachusetts* (Ithaca, 1960); Daniel Scott Smith, "Parental Power and Marriage Patterns: An Analysis of Historical Trends in Hingham, Massachusetts," *Journal of Marriage and the Family* 25 (1973), pp. 419–28.

70. Richard Easterlin, "Factors in the Decline in Farm Family Fertility in the United States: Some Preliminary Research Results," *Journal of American History* 63 (December 1976), pp. 600–14; Ryan, *Cradle of the Middle Class,* chap. 1.

Chapter II

1. Daniel Scott Smith, "Population, Family and Society in Hingham, Massachusetts, 1650 to 1880" (Ph. D. Diss., University of California, Berkeley, 1973).

2. John Hersey, *Advice to Christian Parents* (Baltimore, n.d.), p. 6.

3. Bushnell, *Christian Nurture;* Heman Humphrey, *Domestic Education* (Amherst, 1840), p. 22.

4. Horace Mann, *Lectures on Education* (Boston, 1850), p. 142.

5. John S.C. Abbott, *The Mother at Home* (Boston, 1833), preface.

6. Abbott, *The Child at Home* (New York, 1833), p. 6.

7. Thomas Searle, *A Companion to the Season of Maternal Solicitude* (New York, 1834), p. 81.

8. Ibid., p. 247; John Demos, *The Little Commonwealth* (New York, 1970); David Hunt, *Parents and Children in History* (New York, 1970).

9. Hersey, *Advice to Christian Parents*, p. 78.

10. Ibid., p. 31.

11. Searle, *Companion*, p. 242.

12. Alcott, *Young Man's Guide.*

13. Sedgwick, *Means and Ends of Self-Training* (Boston, 1840), p. 260.

14. Dwight, *The Father's Book*, pp. 113, 192.

15. Thomas Gallaudet, *The Youth's Book on Natural Theology* (New York, 1832), pp. 102–3.

16. Beecher, *Suggestions Respecting Improvements in Education* (Hartford, Conn, 1829), p. 45.

17. Humphrey, *Domestic Education*, pp. 43, 47.

18. Bushnell, *Christian Nurture*, p. 105.

19. Humphrey, *Domestic Duties*, p. 28.

20. Humphrey, *Domestic Duties*, p. 47.

21. Child, *Mother's Book*, p. 26.

22. Humphrey, *Domestic Duties*, p. 184.

23. Alcott, *Observations*, p. 9.

24. Sigourney, *Letters to Mothers* (New York, 1846), p. 32.

25. Child, *Mother's Book*, p. 3.

26. Abbot, *The Mother at Home*, p. 129.

27. Bronson Alcott, *Conversations with Children on the Gospel* (Boston, 1836), pp. xiv, 29, 141.

28. Abbott, *The Child at Home*, pp. 46, 30–31.

29. Sedgwick, *Home*, p. 18.

30. Child, *The Mother's Book*, pp. 28–30; Sigourney, *Letters to Mothers*, p. 44; Andrew Combe, *Treatise on the Physiological and Moral Management of Infancy* (Boston, 1846), pp. 18–19, 247–80.

31. Searle, *Companion*, p. 263.

32. Combe, *Treatise*, p. 249.

33. William Dewees, *A Treatise on the Physical and Medical Treatment of Children* (Philadelphia, 1833), p. 230.

34. Ibid., pp. 245–46; Henry Chavasse, *Advice to Mothers on the Management of Their Offspring* (New York, 1844), pp. 65–67.

35. G. Ackerley, *On the Management of Children in Sickness and Health* (New York, 1831), p. 11.

36. Sigourney, *Letters to Mothers*, p. 9.

37. Abbott, *The Mother at Home*, p. 27; Dewees, *A Treatise*, p. 41; p. 59.

38. Lydia Sigourney, *Poems* (Boston, 1837), p. 10.

39. Sigourney, *Letters to Mothers*, pp. 126–27.

40. Lydia Sigourney, *The Boy's Book* (New York, 1846), pp. 145, 37.

41. Sigourney, *Boy's Book*, pp. 65–72; Louise Hoare, *Hints for the Improvement of Early Education and Nursery Discipline* (London, 1824), p. 101; Mrs. J. Bakewell, *The Mother's Practical Guide in the Early Training of her Children* (New York, 1836), p. 136; Combe, *Treatise*, p. 206.

42. Catharine Maria Sedgwick, *Hope Leslie* (New York, 1827); Sedgwick, *Redwood* (New York, 1824); Lydia Maria Child, *Hobomok* (Boston, 1824); Catharine

Maria Sedgwick, *Clarence* (Philadelphia, 1830), pp. 147, 163; Arthur, *The Mother*, pp. 131–32.

43. Alcott, *The Young Man's Guide;* Alcott, *The Young Husband*, p. 22.

44. Henry Ward Beecher, *Lectures to Young Men* (Boston, 1867), pp. 242, 254, 218.

45. Michael Katz, "Migration and Social Order in Erie County, New York, 1855," *Journal Of Interdisciplinary History* 8, no. 4, (Spring 1978), pp. 669–701; Ryan, *Cradle*, chap. 4.

46. Sedgwick, *Clarence,* pp. 160–63; Smith-Rosenberg, "Female World of Love and Ritual"; Ryan, *Cradle*, chap. 5.

47. Lydia Sigourney, *The Girl's Reading Book* (New York, 1839), p. 8.

48. Mrs. A. J. Graves, *Women in America* (New York, 1855), p. 245; Margaret Graves, *Girlhood and Womanhood* (Boston, 1844), pp. 38–39, vi, Rufus W. Clark, *Lectures to Young Men* (Washington, 1842), p. 67.

49. Herbert Gutman, "The Reality of the Rags-to-Riches 'Myth': The Case of Paterson, New Jersey," in Thernstrom and Sennett, *Nineteenth Century Cities*, pp. 98–125.

50. Fanny Forrester [Emily Chubbuck], "Grace Linden" in *Alderbrook* (Boston, 1849), pp. 7–72.

51. Horace Mann, *A Few Thoughts for Young Men* (Boston, 1850), pp. 57, 5, 7.

52. Beecher, *Lectures*, p. 256.

53. Ibid, pp. 27, 61, 78.

54. Coxe, *Claims of the Country*, pp. 191, 204; Arthur, *The Mother*, chap. 12.

55. Child, *The Mother's Book*, p. 141.

56. Forrester, *Alderbrook*, p. 37.

57. Lucius M. Sargent, "Margaret's Bridal," in *The Temperance Tale* (Boston, 1853), pp. 253–83.

58. Alice Carey, "The Convict," in *The National Temperance Offering* (New York, 1850), pp. 18–21.

59. Arthur, "The Circean Cup" in Ibid., pp. 79–102.

60. Lydia Sigourney, "Louise Wilson," in *Water Drops* (New York, 1848), pp. 87–119.

61. Timothy Shay Arthur, *Six Nights with the Washingtonians* (Philadelphia, 1871), pp. 82–88.

62. Arthur, *Temperance Tales* (Philadelphia, 1848), pp. 1–45.

63. John R. Gough, *Platform Echoes* (Hartford, 1894), pp. 236–37; Lucius Sargent, *The Stage Coach* (Boston, 1863), pp. 196–258.

64. Gough, *Platform Echoes*, p. 187.

65. Arthur, *Six Nights*, p. 72.

66. Forrester, *Alderbrook,* pp. 258–74.

67. Timothy Shay Arthur, *Ten Nights in a Bar Room* (Cambridge, Mass., 1964), pp. 154–55.

68. Lydia Sigourney, *The Faded Hope* (New York, 1853), pp. 47, 67, 94.

69. Ibid., pp. 247, 212, 222–23.

70. Ibid., p. 244.

Chapter III

1. Kate Barclay, *The Temperance Token* (Geneva, New York, 1847), p. 21.

2. *Permanent Temperance Documents of the American Temperance Society*, vol. 1 (Boston, 1835), pp. 429, 265.

3. Ibid., pp. 59–60, 154–55.

4. *Permanent Temperance Documents*, vol. 1, pp. 129, 130–31, 321.

5. Ibid., "Fifth Annual Report," p. 3.

6. Ibid., "Sixth Annual Report," pp. 13–18.

7. Arthur, *Six Nights with the Washingtonians,* pp. 39–40.

8. Ibid.

9. Carroll Smith-Rosenberg, "Beauty, the Beast, and the Militant Woman: A Case Study in Sex Roles and Social Stress in Jacksonian America," *American Quarterly* 23 (1971): pp. 562–84; Berg, *The Remembered Gate.*

10. *Advocate of Moral Reform,* September 15, 1837.

11. Ibid., September 15, 1840.

12. Ibid.

13. Ibid., 4 (August 1838); for recent interpretations of ante-bellum utopias see Lawrence Foster, *Religion and Sexuality: Three American Communal Experiments in the Nineteenth Century* (New York, 1981); and Louis Kern *An Ordered Love: Sex Roles and Sexuality in Victorian Utopias* (Chapel Hill, N.C., 1981).

14. Sams, *Autobiography of Brook Farm,* p. 25.

15. John Humphrey Noyes, *History of American Socialism* (New York, 1870), p. 292.

16. Hubbard Eastman, *Noyesism Unveiled* (Brattleboro, Vt., 1849), pp. 20, 27, 403.

17. *Second Annual Report of the Oneida Association* (Oneida, N.Y., 1850), p. 18.

18. Noyes, *History,* p. 268.

19. Ibid., pp. 416–21.

20. *Mind Amongst the Spindle: Selections from the Lowell Offering* (London, 1845), p. 192.

21. Eastman, *Noyesism Unveiled,* p. 395.

22. *The Witness,* 1, (January 1839), p. 56; *The Witness,* 1 (January 1840), pp. 102–3.

23. Ibid. 1 (March 1839), p. 56, and (January 1840), pp. 102–3.

24. Sedgwick, *Redwood,* p. 283; Sedgwick, Diary, September 18, 1827, Sedgwick Papers MHS.

25. Albert Brisbane, *The Social Destiny of Man* (New York, 1968), p. 132.

26. Henry W. Sams, ed., *Autobiography of Brook Farm,* (Englewood Cliffs, N.J., 1958), pp. 3, 6.

27. Fayette Mace, *Familiar Dialogues on Shakerism* (Portland, 1838), pp. 69, 70.

28. Franklin Evans, *Autobiography of a Shaker and Revelation of the Apocalypse* (New York, 1869), pp. 16ff.

29. Noyes, *History,* pp. 137–38.

30. Ibid., p. 138.

31. *Witness,* 1 (August 1837), p. 1.

32. Evans, *Autobiography of a Shaker,* preface.

33. Ibid., pp. 46–47.

34. *Second Annual Report of the Oneida Association,* p. 13.

35. *First Annual Report of the Oneida Association* (Oneida, N.Y., 1847), p. 7.

36. Mary Dyer Marshall, *The Rise and Progress of the Serpent* (Concord, 1847), p. 177.

37. Eastman, *Noyesism Unveiled,* p. 276.

38. Brisbane, *Social Destiny of Man,* p. 431.

39. *Harbinger* 2 (May 23, 1846).

40. [Rufus Bishop and Others], *Juvenile Guide or Manual of Good Manners* (Canterbury, 1844).

41. Brisbane, *Social Destiny of Man.*

42. Hervey Elkins, *Fifteen Years in the Senior Order of Shaker* (Hanover, N.H., 1853), pp. 104–6.

43. Noyes, *The Berean* (Putney, Vt., 1847), pp. 246–52.

44. Maren Lockwood Carden, *Oneida: Utopian Community to Modern Corpora-tion* (Baltimore, 1969), pp. 33–34.
45. *Autobiography of Brook Farm,* pp. 132, 195.
46. *Harbinger,* 1 (September 27, 1845), pp. 252–53.
47. *Autobiography of Brook Farm,* pp. 132, 195.
48. *First Report of Oneida Association,* pp. 43–50.
49. *The Witness,* 1 (January 1839), p. 6.
50. Noyes, *Male Continence* (Oneida, 1872), pp. 13–14.
51. Ibid.
52. Lewis S. Hough, *The Science of Man* (Boston, 1849), Lecture 4, pp. 125–73.
53. Elkins, *Fifteen Years,* pp. 4–5.
54. Ibid., pp. 135–36.
55. Mace, *Familiar Dialogues,* p. 22.
56. *Witness,* 2 (November 1842), pp. 164–65.
57. Brisbane, *Social Destiny of Man,* p. 299.
58. *Harbinger,* 4 (February 13, 1847), p. 158.
59. Ibid., 3 (September 26, 1846), p. 253.
60. *Autobiography of Brook Farm,* p. 35.
61. Elkins, *Fifteen Years,* p. 27.
62. Bishop, *Juvenile Guide,* pp. 4–7.
63. *Perfectionist,* 3 (January 1844), p. 87.
64. *Juvenile Guide,* passim.
65. Eastman, *Noyesism Unveiled,* p. 179.
66. Ibid.
67. Brisbane, *Social Destiny of Man,* chap. 31.
68. *Harbinger,* 1 (July 12, 1845), pp. 70–72; *Harbinger,* 1 (September 27, 1845), pp. 251–52.
69. Noyes, *History,* p. 520.
70. Ibid., p. 27.
71. Ibid., pp. 194–95.
72. John Marsh, "A Half Century Tribute to the Temperance Cause," in *Perma-nent Temperance Documents,* vol. 3 (New York, 1851), p. 18.

Chapter IV

1. Henry C. Wright, *Marriage and Parentage* (Boston, 1855), p. 300.
2. Henry C. Wright, *The Empire of the Mother* (Boston, 1870), p. 27.
3. Alfred Donne, *Mothers and Infants, Nurses and Nursing* (Boston, 1859), "Translator's Preface."
4. Catharine Beecher, *A Treatise on Domestic Economy* (New York, 1850), p. 5.
5. Elizabeth Peabody, *Guide to Kindergarten and Intermediate Class* (New York, 1877), p. 38.
6. Wright, *The Empire,* p. 5.
7. Donne, *Mothers and Infants,* pp. 3, 35.
8. Orson S. Fowler, *Maternity* (New York, 1855), p. 206.
9. Thomas L. Nichols, *Esoteric Anthropology* (London, n.d.), p. 321.
10. Peabody, *Kindergarten Guide,* pp. 12–13.
11. Ibid., p. 39.
12. Ibid., p. 54–57.
13. Ibid., p. 53.
14. Ibid., p. 43.

15. Mary Mann, *Moral Culture of Infancy* (New York, 1877), pp. 158, 188–89.
16. Michael Katz, *The Irony of Early School Reform* (Cambridge, Mass., 1968), pp. 42–43.
17. David Rothman, *The Discovery of Asylums* (Boston, 1971), p. 235.
18. Katz, *The Irony*, p. 193; Robert Ernst, *Immigrant Life in New York City* (New York, 1945), p. 179.
19. Peabody, *Kindergarten Guide*, p. 3.
20. Lydia Maria Child, *Flowers for Children* (Boston, 1864), pp. 177–8.
21. Harriet Beecher Stowe, *Our Charley* (Boston, 1858).
22. Ralph Waldo Emerson, "Domestic Life" in *The Works of Ralph Waldo Emerson*, vol. 7 (Boston, 1898), pp. 99–129.
23. Stowe, *Our Charley*, p. 8.
24. Bernard Wishey, *The Child and the Republic* (Philadelphia, 1968).
25. Timothy Shay Arthur, *The Angel of the Household* (Philadelphia, 1854).
26. Wright, *Empire*, p. 5.
27. Orson S. Fowler, *Creative and Sexual Science* (New York, 1870), p. 326.
28. Thomas L. Nichols and Mary Gove Nichols, *Marriage, Its History, Character and Results* (Cincinatti, 1855), p. 307.
29. Nichols, *Esoteric Anthropology*, p. 100.
30. R.T. Trall, *Sexual Physiology* (New York, 1866), p. 136.
31. Paul David and Warren Sanderson, "The Effectiveness of Nineteenth Century Contraceptive Practices," pp. 67–68.
32. Nichols, *Esoteric Anthropology*, p. 42.
33. Fowler, *Creative and Sexual Science*, pp. 620–21.
34. Nichols, *Esoteric Anthropology*, p. 101.
35. Alcott, *Moral Philosophy*, pp. 61–68.
36. Wright, *Reproductive Element*, p. 74.
37. Wright, *Marriage and Parentage*, p. 289.
38. Nichols, *Marriage*, p. 309.
39. M. Edgworth Lazarus, *Love versus Marriage* (New York, 1852), p. 26.
40. Stephen Pearl Andrews, *Love, Marriage, and Divorce* (Boston, 1889), p. 88.
41. Ibid., p. 36.
42. Wright, *Marriage and Parentage*, p. 308.
43. Elizabeth Cady Stanton, Susan B. Anthony and Matilda Cage, *History of Woman's Suffrage* (New York, 1881), pp. 720, 729.
44. Wright, *Marriage and Parentage*, p. 302.
45. Gervase Wheeler, *Homes for the People* (New York, 1855), p. 260.
46. Fowler, *A Home for All* (New York, 1855), pp. 8–9.
47. Wheeler, *Rural Homes* (New York, 1855), p. 3.
48. Andrew Jackson Downing, *Architecture of Country Houses* (New York, 1850), p. 257.
49. Wheeler, *Homes for the People*, pp. 289–90; Cleaveland and Backas Architects, *Village and Farm Cottages* (New York, 1857), p. iii; Fowler, *A Home for All*, p. iii.
50. Charles J. Kennedy, "Commuter Services in the Boston Area, 1835–1860," *Business History Review* 36 (Summer 1962), pp. 153–70; Sam Bass Warner, *Streetcar Suburbs* (Cambridge, Mass., 1962).
51. *Village and Farm Cottages*, p. 12.
52. Ibid.
53. Andrew Jackson Downing, *Cottage Residences* (New York, 1842), pp. iii–iv.
54. Downing, *Architecture for Country Houses*, p. vi.
55. Fowler, *A Home for All*, p. 97; Wheeler, *Rural Homes*, p. 22.
56. *Village and Farm Cottages*, p. 157.

57. Ibid., p. 115.

58. Wright, *Marriage and Parentage*, p. 310.

59. Downing, *Architecture of Country Houses*, p. 407.

60. Dorothy Brady, "Relative Prices in the Nineteenth Century," *Journal of Economic History* 24 (June 1964), pp. 45–204.

61. *The Lily*, 4 (January, 1852), p. 3; *The Lily*, 7 (November, 1855), p. 168; *The Lily*, 7 (August, 1855), p. 119.

62. *The Lily*, 7 (August, 1855), p. 110.

63. Ernestine Rose, "Speech at Woman's Rights Convention in Syracuse, 1852," in *Woman's Rights Tracts* (Syracuse, 1853), p. 6.

64. Lucretia Mott, *Discourse on Woman* (Philadelphia, 1850), p. 15.

65. Stanton, *History of Woman's Suffrage*, p. 669.

66. Sarah Grimke to Ellis Gray Loring, February 10, 1856, in Lydia Maria Child Papers, New York Public Library (hereafter, NYPL).

67. Lazarus, *Love versus Marriage*, p. 91.

68. Horace Mann, *A Few Thoughts on the Power and Duties of Woman*, (Syracuse, N.Y., 1853), p. 125.

69. Lydia Sigourney, "Introduction," to J. Clement ed., *Noble Deeds of American Women* (Buffalo, 1851), pp. xx–xxi.

70. Emerson, "Woman," in *Works*, vol. 8, p. 340.

71. Mann, *A Few Thoughts on the Power and Duties of Women*. p. 99.

72. Alcott, *Courtship and Marriage*, p. 164.

73. Alexis de Tocqueville, *Democracy in America* (New York, 1945), p. 105.

Chapter V

1. Hellmut Lehmann-Haupt, *The Book in America* (New York, 1951), p. 72; William Charvat, *Literary Publishing in America* (Philadelphia, 1959), p. 22.

2. James D. Hart, *The Popular Book* (New York, 1950), pp. 20, 86.

3. Helen Papashvily, *All the Happy Endings* (New York, 1956), pp. 1–2.

4. Lydia Sigourney to Theodore Dwight, January 29, 1833, Sigourney Papers, NYPL.

5. Lydia Child to Louisa Loring, January 1, 1868, Loring Family Papers, Schlesinger Library, Radcliffe College (hereafter SL).

6. Lydia Child to R.W. Griswold, May 1, 1843, Griswold Papers, Boston Public Library (hereafter BPL).

7. Catharine Sedgwick to Kate Minot, March 8, 1837, Sedgwick Papers, MHS.

8. Catharine Sedgwick to William Minot, July 20, 1857, Sedgwick Papers MHS.

9. Lydia Sigourney to Robert Bonner, July 20, 1857, Sedgwick Papers, MHS.

10. Papashvily, *All the Happy Endings*, pp. 64–74.

11. Ibid., pp. 110–21.

12. Lydia Child to Maria Weston Chapman, August 23, 1840, Weston Papers, BPL.

13. Lydia Sigourney to Mary A. Patrick, February 14, 1840, Sigourney Papers, Columbia University Library Special Collections (hereafter CSC).

14. Ann Douglas Wood, "Mrs. Sigourney and the Sensibility of the Inner Space," *New England Quarterly* 45 (June 1972), pp. 163–81.

15. Lydia Child to E.G. Loring September 28, 1841 and August 11, 1841, Child Papers, NYPL.

16. Catharine Sedgwick, Diary, June 29, 1828, Sedgwick Papers, MHS.

17. Lydia Child to Maria Weston Chapman, August 23, 1840, Weston Papers, BPL.

18. Catharine Sedgwick, *Married or Single* (Philadelphia, 1855), pp. 12, 284.

19. Timothy Shay Arthur, *Married and Single* (Philadelphia, 1855), p. 12.

20. Marion Harland [Mary Virginia Hawes], *Alone,* (New York, 1854), pp. 381–84.

21. Augusta Jane Evans, *Beulah,* (New York, 1859), p. 500.

22. Emma D.E.N. Southworth, *The Curse of Clifton* (Philadelphia, 1875), pp. 464, 466.

23. Timothy Shay Arthur, *What Can a Woman Do?* (New York, 1856), p. 82.

24. Charles W. Webber, *Tales of the Southern Border* (Philadelphia, 1852), p. 208.

25. Arthur, *What Can a Woman Do?*, p. 325–36; Arthur, *Lovers and Husbands* (Philadelphia, 1855), p. 136.

26. Fanny Fern [Sarah Payson Willis], *Fern Leaves from Fanny's Portfolio* (Buffalo, 1853), pp. 346–47, 324.

27. Ibid., pp. 378, 363, 398.

28. Ike Marvel [Daniel Mitchell], *Reveries of a Bachelor* (New York, 1907), p. 151.

29. George P. Curtis, *Prue and I* (London, 1892), p. 80.

30. Daniel Mitchell, *Dream Life* (New York, 1907), p. 105.

31. Susan Warner, *The Wide Wide World* (New York, 1902).

32. Maria Cummins, *The Lamplighter* (New York, 1897).

33. Elizabeth Smith, *The Newsboy* (New York, 1854), pp. 169, 320.

34. Anne S. Stephens, *Fashion and Famine* (New York, 1854), p. 294.

35. Ibid., p. 177.

36. Webber, *Tales of the Southern Border,* pp. 9–44, 121–51.

37. Herman Melville, *Pierre* (New York, Signet Paperback Edition, 1964), p. 403.

38. Ibid., p. 215.

39. Ibid., p. 135.

40. Ibid., p. 25.

41. Ibid., p. 351.

42. Ibid., p. 207.

43. Ibid., p. 93.

44. Ibid., p. 341.

45. Ibid., p. 56–58.

46. Timothy Shay Arthur, *Homelights and Shadows* (New York, 1853), p. iii.

47. Grace Greenwood [Sara Clark], *Greenwood Leaves* (Boston, 1850), chap. 2.

48. Caroline Gilman, *Recollections of a Southern Matron* (New York, 1837), pp. 235–36; John Pendleton Kennedy, *Swallowbarn* (New York, 1851), pp. 461–90; Sarah Josepha Hale, *Northwood* (New York, 1852), pp. 121–22; William R. Taylor, *Cavalier and Yankee* (New York, 1961); Richard Hildreth, *The Slave* (New York, 1836), vol. 1, p. 6; vol. 2, p. 9.

49. *The Liberator,* 1, January 1, 1831, p. 1.

50. Ibid; *The Poetical Works of Elizabeth Margaret Chandler* (Philadelphia, 1837).

51. Thornton Randolph [Charles Jacobs Peterson], *The Cabin and the Parlor* (Philadelphia, 1852), pp. 124–25.

52. Caroline Lee Hentz, *The Planter's Northern Bride* (Philadelphia, 1851), pp. vii–viii; Stowe, *Uncle Tom's Cabin* (New York, Colliers Paperback Edition, 1962), pp. 294–308.

53. Hentz, *Planter's Northern Bride,* p. 206; Maria McIntosh, *The Lofty and the Lowly* (New York, 1852), pp. 5–6; Mary H. Eastman, *Aunt Phillus's Cabin* (Philadelphia, 1852), passim.

54. Stowe, *Uncle Tom,* pp. 69–73.

55. Ibid., p. 88.

56. Ibid., p. 325.

57. Hentz, *Planter's Northern Bride,* p. 457.

58. Ibid., p. 282.

59. McIntosh, *Lofty and Lowly,* chap. 1.

60. Peterson, *Cabin and Parlor,* p. 241.

61. Ibid., p. 171.

62. Ibid., p. 180.

63. Lydia Sigourney to Mary Patrick, November 24, 1860, Sigourney Papers MHS; Catharine Sedgwick to Kate Minot, November 6, 1859, Sedgwick Papers MHS.

64. Lydia Child, fragment of letter, 1856, Loring Family Papers, SL.

65. Child to Anna Loring, February 27, 1860, Loring Family Papers, SL.

66. McIntosh, *Lofty and Lowly,* pp. 311–12; for a description of the wider networks among slaves, see Herbert Gutman, *The Black Family in Slavery and Freedom* (New York, 1976), especially chaps. 3, 4, 5.

67. Stowe, *Uncle Tom,* pp. 490–91.

68. Ibid., p. 44.

69. Charles K. Whipple, *The Family Relationship as Affected by Slavery* (Cincinatti, 1858), p. 13.

70. Ibid., pp. 14–15, 20.

71. Ibid., p. 23.

72. Lydia Maria Child, *The Patriarchal Institution* (New York, 1860), pp. 50–52.

INDEX

Abbott, John S. C., 47,52,57; *The Child at Home,* 53
abortionists, 29
Adams, Nehemiah, 20,23,29
adolescence, 57,59; adolescent identity formation, 59; adolescent dilemma, 91
adult, 82; adulthood, 59–60
Advocate of Moral Reform; 76–79; "Mother's Department," 78; domestic ideology, 79; as ladies' magazine, 94; Harriet Beecher Stowe, 132. *See also* American Female Moral Reform Society.
"Affection," 32
agricultural production, 13
alcoholism, 91; professionals and, 92. *See also* intemperance.
Alcott, A(mos) Bronson, 46, 50–51; *Conversations with Children on the Gospel,* 52
Alcott, William Andros, 20,21,24–25,26,30,32,37,46,51,59,61,83,89,113; courtship and marriage, 98; definition of marriage, 26,29; on keeping a daily journal, 49; marriage of companionship, 105; merchant capitalist, 61; on mate selection, 28; "partner in trade," 26; S. J. Hale on, 34, *see also* Hale, S. J.; on sexual relations, 28
Alderbrook, 68; Robert Flemming, 68
American Enlightenment, 49–50
American Female Moral Reform Society, 76–77
American Revolution, 7,14; Revolutionary era, 72
American Temperance Society (1826), Permanent Temperance Documents, 73. *See also* Beecher, L.
American Temperance Union (1833),

72–77; partial vs. total abstinence, 74
Andrews, Stephen Pearl, essence of free love, 106–107; debate with Greeley, 107
ante-bellum, 7,9,14,17,45,49,60,63,72, 79,146; Americans and geographic and economic dislocation, 16; women, decline of fertility in, 2; domesticity, 1,2,143, (dialectic of) 79; publishers, 14; women and docility, 2; women's fiction, 2; women's movement, 5; writers, 10,45,57–58
ante-bellum architecture; architects, 108; and domestic home, 108; for middle-class, 108; "suburban cottages," 109
Appalachians, 13
Arthur, T. S., 34–35,46,75; "Angel of the Household," 103; "The Circean Cup," 65; *Home Lights and Shadows,* 129; *Married and Single;* The Mother, 35, (the Hartlys) 35, Mary Hartly 61,38,63; *Six Nights with the Washingtonians,* 66,67; *Ten Nights in a Bar Room,* 68–69, (William Hammond) 68; "What Can a Woman Do," 122
At Odds, see Degler, Carl

Baltimore, 34; Washingtonians, 74
bankruptcy, 62; and intemperance, 66
Baptist, 21
Barclay(s), *see* Sedgewick, C. *Home*
Baum, Nina, 2
Beecher, Catharine, 2,21,22,25,34,36, 40,46,50,59; domestic ennui and idleness, 36; on child-rearing, 68
Beecher, Henry Ward, 59–60, 132; on bankruptcy, 62; "Relations to Employers," 62

161